Off-Limits Grumpy Doctor

An Enemies to Lovers Boss Romance

Brandy Piker

Contents

Chapter One

♥

Lilian

A sudden screeching sound jolts me back to the present and I look down to see the bumper of a blue Bentley just inches away from my body.

My heart is pounding furiously in my chest. I'm still trying to process the fact that I just narrowly escaped being flung across the sidewalk when a man appears in front of me. He appears menacingly tall compared to my five feet six inches.

He has the bluest eyes I've ever looked into and looks like he just walked off a runway in Milan. His sandy brown hair—which in my opinion has way too much hair gel—glistens in the evening sun.

Were he not presently yelling at me, I would spend the next few minutes imagining what our babies would look like.

"Are you out of your mind? How could you just step into the road without looking?" His deep baritone voice, smooth like velvet, booms through the air.

"Would you give me a break? I'm having a terrible day as it is."

"One that would've gotten a lot worse for the both of us had I run you over. You need to be more careful next time."

"Oh please, you would've seen me if you weren't barreling down the road like a lunatic," I retort defensively.

His eyes flare up. "Unbelievable! You're lucky I slammed the brakes when I did or we would be having a very different conversation right now."

"Lucky? Oh no, mister, you're the lucky one. I would've sued the pants off you had you given me so much as a scratch."

"Next time use the sidewalk, moron," he says, walking back to his car.

"And learn to control your temper, psycho," I call out to him as he zooms off.

Great, I haven't even been back one minute and the streak of bad luck continues.

For the first time since I got off the train from New York, I look around me, trying to savor the view of my hometown, but my despondency makes me feel nothing.

My older brother Aiden, who had promised to come pick me up from the train station, called last minute to say he couldn't make it because his car had broken down on the way.

I don't mind, seeing as I'm in no hurry to get home. As a matter of fact, I wouldn't be returning home at all if I had a choice in the matter—the Big Apple chewed me up and spit me out like tasteless gum, and I'm headed home to lick my wounds.

Last month made it nine years since I left Elvesridge to live with Aunt Betty, my mom's younger sister, and attend Columbia University—home to one of the most prestigious medical schools in America.

Two years in, Aunt Betty and her husband Paul split after five years of marriage and she decided to move back home. Unlike me, who had been eager to see how the other half lived in the big city, she loved Elvesridge and had only left because of Paul.

I used the money I had saved up to get an apartment, found a roommate, and spent the next six years chasing a dream that would come crashing down like a house of cards.

Now I'm back, breathing in the familiar scent of freshly baked pastries coming from Ida Sue's bakery—frankly, I'm shocked the bakery is still standing because it's like a million years old.

As I contemplate whether to take a taxi or wait for the bus, I hear a familiar voice behind me.

"Look who the cat dragged in."

Turning around, I see Aiden standing beside his sea-green Chevrolet, a car he's had since he started driving and probably loves more than any of his numerous girlfriends. With his chin-length hair—*dark blond just like mine*—flowing down his face, he looks like an old Hollywood movie star.

"Come on, I don't look that bad, do I?" I ask when I reach his car.

"You look terrible."

"And you're an ass. You told me your car broke down and you couldn't pick me up."

"Please. My little not-so-little sister is coming home from the big city for the first time in nine years and you believed I wouldn't be here to pick you up? I'm not *that* much of an ass," he says, bringing me into a hug. "Welcome home, baby sis."

I stay in the hug a little longer than usual, happy to finally be in a place that feels somewhat familiar and safe after the rough patches I've been through lately. Aiden, in his usual way, lets me, understanding that I need the hug.

Eventually, I pull away and he takes my suitcases and puts them in his trunk.

"So how are Mom and Dad handling my homecoming, I hope they're not making it that big a deal?" I ask Aiden, fumbling with my seat belt as he pulls onto the road.

"Are you kidding me?" He takes his eyes off the road to shoot me a glance. "You think they'll be mellow about you coming home after nine years?"

"Oh God, what did they do?"

"It's supposed to be a surprise, but tons of our family and friends are waiting to welcome you when we get home so you better act surprised or Mom will kill me."

"Damn it! I told them several times that I wanted a quiet homecoming."

"Mom and Dad didn't listen to what someone else wanted? Surprise, surprise. Plus, Aunt Florence has been so eager for your return she would've thrown the surprise party herself if they hadn't."

"Oh no." I lean my head against the side window. "Aunt Flo is gonna be there? Here come the *when are you bringing a decent man home to us* questions."

"You won't believe how much she's been on my case. She introduces me to a daughter of one of her friends every other week."

"Could you sneak me in through the back, or better still drive me back to New York?"

Aiden lets out a laugh, loud and throaty. One I realize I've missed hearing. "I'm afraid I won't be able to help you with that."

I fall silent, mentally preparing myself to meet with my overzealous family on a day I absolutely do not want their zeal. Spending the entire ride home rehearsing how not to have a resting bitch face when I see their enthusiastic faces is a more difficult task than I imagined.

Soon, we pull onto the narrow dirt road leading to the Weatherby Mansion, one of the oldest houses in Elvesridge. Our third great-grandfather George built it in 1920, three years after he moved to America from Ireland and married my third great-grandmother Pamela Hutchins.

We pass a wooden arrow with *Weatherby Mansion* written on it, and Aiden pulls onto the short cobblestone driveway. The mansion is standing there in all its cream-colored glory, front held up by two big white columns, tall oaks casting their shadows over the manicured lawns.

"Home sweet home," I sigh sarcastically, stepping out of the car.

As we walk up to the double mahogany door—the polished glossy finish gleaming in the evening sun—I take a deep breath and push it open, expecting a deafening yell of *Surprise!* to fill the air. Instead, I see Mom and Dad, standing there alone, huge smiles plastered across their faces.

I turn to Aiden and he flashes me a mischievous smile. Aiden the prankster. He got me again.

"Hi Mom, hi Dad," I say, recovering from, well—not being surprised.

"Honey, we look almost the same age and you're so skinny," Mom says, looking me up and down. "What were they feeding you in New York?"

"Gee, thanks, Mom. Way to make a girl feel good about herself."

Dad pulls me into a bear hug. "Don't mind your mom, sweetheart. You look great, and it's really good to have you home."

Mom smiles and takes my hand in hers. "Of course, baby. We're glad you're back where you belong."

More like where failing has forced me to belong, I think to myself.

Looking around, I ask, "Where's everyone?"

Despite my quiet welcome being just what I had hoped for, it's very strange to see the house so quiet and deserted.

"They went to help Lucy Bunch with some repairs on her ranch. Last week's storm, terrible as it was, destroyed her barns and stables. Your brother and dad would be there right now had you not been coming home today."

The sense of community is one thing I definitely missed about Elvesridge. Even though I'm not feeling very communal these days, it's still better than New York where you could go for years without knowing who lives next door to you.

"Aiden, honey, take your sister's bags to her room." Mom turns to me. "Everything is still just as you left it. You need to freshen up and come down for some proper food."

Aiden leads the way, hauling my suitcases up the stairs so casually, like they don't contain my whole life.

Mom wasn't kidding when she said the room was exactly how I left it. After nine years, I expected a few things to have been moved around, but aside from the regular cleaning that my mom would have insisted the housekeepers do, everything else is the same.

My Mariah Carey and Celine Dion posters still hang on the wall, a modified image of me and Justin Bieber kinda kissing hanging in between them.

Don't judge me, I was sixteen at the time and had caught the Belieber fever.

"So no one took my room, huh?"

Aiden leans against the portion of my wall that I painted blood red when I went through my creepy vampire phase. *Still sixteen, people! Okay, maybe I was seventeen. Let's just excuse it as teenage silliness.*

"Not for a lack of trying, but Mom remained adamant that no one was going to occupy it."

"Almost as if she knew I would fail and come back home."

Aiden gives me a knowing glance. "I'm sure that wasn't it."

He's the only one in my life who knows why I really came home. I fed everyone else some bullshit story about being overworked in the big city and needing a break.

Opening my closet, I find that all my clothes are still neatly arranged, just like they were the day I left.

"I need to keep busy or I'm going to drive myself crazy," I say, shutting the closet door.

"Maybe you should get a job. I hear Ida Sue needs help at her bakery, or you could work at Lucy's ranch."

"Look at me, bro. Do I look like I'm cut out for baking or parking horseshit?"

Aiden's phone beeps and he pulls it out and responds to what I'm guessing is a text.

"Sorry, that was my friend Levi. You remember him, don't you?"

I shake my head no.

"His father used to run Greenwood Hospital but he took over a year ago."

"Yeah, I remember Dr. Greenwood. He used to treat me when I was little, but I'm not so sure I remember his son. How close are you two?"

"Very."

"And he runs the hospital now?"

"Yeah."

"That's awesome."

"Why is that awesome?" Aiden asks, a suspicious look on his face.

"If it's not too much for me to ask, could you put in a good word for me? A job at a hospital is just what I need right now."

"I'll try, but there are no guarantees. Levi is a little wound up when it comes to matters concerning that hospital. Besides, are you sure you're up for this, after what happened?"

"God no. That's why I'll be applying as a physician's assistant."

"Alright then, I'll talk to him and I'll leave you to freshen up."

After Aiden leaves, I sink into the pristinely made king-sized bed and curl into the fetal position. With my family's influence and affluence, I need only wave a finger and a thousand positions would be made available to me. But I don't want to work for any member of my family, especially not for my mom.

She always thought I would become a dentist like her and Grandma, so she was devastated when I chose another medical field as my path.

Despite what Aiden says, being in this room right now makes me feel like she was patiently waiting for me to fail, come home, and beg her for a position at the clinic, and by God, I'm not going to give her the satisfaction.

I pull out my phone and open Instagram, then go straight to Kelsey Carter's IG to sulk over her getting my dream job at Mount Sinai Hospital.

Sending in my application to Mount Sinai and being rejected was the catalyst that pushed me to finally give up on New York and return home, my tail between my legs. And now, seeing a picture of Kelsey in her hospital scrubs, her ID tag pinned to her chest, feels like a dagger piercing through my heart.

Thank God for Aiden and his friend's hospital. I'm keeping my fingers crossed that there'll be a position for me there and I won't spend my days in bed pining over what could have been.

Chapter Two

♥

Levi

"Dr. Close, is the patient's head secure?"

"Yes, Dr. Greenwood."

"Scalpel please." I put out my hand and one of the scrub nurses, Jolie, hands it to me.

Normally Jolie shouldn't be the one handing me the scalpel but my assistant Scott quit on me a week ago, as soon as he got a job offer from a hospital in Dallas.

The wimp didn't even have the good sense to wait till after one of the toughest weeks of my career.

"I'm making a horseshoe incision on the scalp now," I say, carefully cutting through the tissues of the scalp before handing the scalpel back to the nurse.

"Now I'm using the high-speed drill to drill some holes around the perimeter of the bone flap. Next is the rongeur, which I'm going to use to shape and cut the bone."

After cutting the bone, Jolie places the bone elevator in my outstretched hand and I use it to gently lift and separate the bone flap from the protective covering of the brain.

"Who knows what we need to do next?"

"We'll use a suction device to remove bone dust and debris from the surgical site so you can have a clear view of the area," Dr. Turner, one of my attendings, responds.

"Excellent," I say, nodding in agreement.

"Now it's time to remove the blood clots and stop the bleeding. I will use the neuroendoscope to find out the exact location of the blood clots within the brain so I can remove them without damaging surrounding tissue. How's the patient's heart rate and blood pressure?"

"Stable, Dr. Greenwood," my surgical nurse, Phil, replies.

"How about her oxygen levels?"

"Oxygen levels are normal."

"Alright, let's proceed. Next, I need some dissectors to separate some of the brain tissue and allow me direct access to the blood clots. Dr. Turner, grab the forceps and clamp down on this blood vessel here."

"Done."

"I'm removing the blood clots now. There are several visible blood clots in the patient's brain, so I'm going to very carefully take them out, one after the other, to avoid damage to any neighboring tissue."

After I've removed all the visible blood clots and made sure there's no bleeding, I call for screws and wires to reposition the part of the scalp I removed earlier.

"And now for the final step. I'm going to reposition all the soft tissues and muscles I dissected during the initial scalp incision and suture them closed," I announce to the hearing of everyone in the operating room.

As I suture, I take care to ensure I provide an aesthetically pleasing closure.

"And...done," I announce as I close the last stitch and cut the excess wires.

"Fantastic suture, Dr. Greenwood."

"Thank you, Dr. Close. Time?"

"One hour, sixteen minutes," Jolie answers, looking at the stopwatch.

"Ladies and gentlemen, we have successfully finished our eleventh mock craniotomy without any incidents, fatal or otherwise. I believe we are ready to handle our real patient tomorrow afternoon. This simulation may have taken us about an hour and sixteen minutes but we all know the actual surgery can take anywhere between two to eight hours due to many factors. I advise that everyone should get some proper rest when they get home tonight."

"Okay, Dr. Greenwood," they respond in unison.

"Once again, well done, team," I say, pushing open the revolving doors of the operating room.

'Very nicely done, Dr. Greenwood," Dr. Thorne, my second-in-command and one of the best doctors in Greenwood Hospital tells me as I take off my mask and gloves.

She was watching me from the viewing center.

"Thanks, Dr. Thorne."

If I had my way, she would be in the OR with me tomorrow, but I need a doctor competent enough to handle any other emergency that arises in the hospital without needing to consult me, to be in charge tomorrow while I undergo the biggest surgical test of my entire career.

"There's something I want to discuss with you. It's about—"

"Is it a life or death situation?"

"Not really, but—"

"Then it can wait. I want to go address Mayor Wembley and his family now. Dr. Close, come with me."

Dr. Close and I take the elevator to the hospital's third floor which is also the VIP ward. On getting to Mayor Wembley's daughter's room, I see the mayor and Agatha, his wife, who have refused to leave their daughter's side since we induced her coma to reduce the swelling in her brain.

Despite my many assurances that she is in good hands and they could go home for a few hours, the mayor and his wife have stayed put.

Priscilla Wembley, the mayor's seventeen-year-old daughter, was on a ski trip with some of her friends two towns over when she collided with another skier, fell off her skis, and hit her head on a rock resulting in a traumatic brain injury.

Thinking quickly, the people present had rushed her to the town's hospital, but when the mayor found out he arranged for her to be transferred to Greenwood as soon as she was stable enough to travel.

"How are you all doing today?" I ask, forcing a smile to mask my rattling nerves.

"We'll be much better when you tell us how our girl is doing."

"This is my colleague Dr. Ben Close. He used to work closely with my father until he retired."

"Hi Dr. Close," the Wembleys greet him before I continue.

"From the MRI scans we did, the swelling in her brain no longer seems to be increasing, but the problem is that it's not decreasing either. We also found some blood clots in the brain which means a craniotomy is still our only option. We need to relieve the swelling in her brain and remove the blood clots."

The mayor looks at his wife and I see fear pass between them.

"Dr. Greenwood, she's our only child. I'm not sure my wife and I can bear to lose her."

On the inside, I'm kinda freaking out, but my exterior remains as calm as a millpond.

"Mayor and Mrs. Wembley…"

"You can call us Saul and Agatha," he offers.

"Saul, Agatha, I understand your concerns and I will not sugarcoat things by telling you the surgery isn't risky. It is very risky and your daughter has a forty to sixty percent chance of coming out of the OR alive and with her brain functions intact. However, she will have a zero percent chance of survival if we don't perform the craniotomy by tomorrow afternoon. In fact, the only reason we're waiting till afternoon is so that we can administer some mannitol and see if the swelling can go down any further."

"Have you ever done a surgery like this before?" Mayor Wembley asks, his voice a little shaky.

"While I haven't performed this surgery on a human patient before, I have closely watched and assisted my father with it multiple times and I am confident that I can do it. Plus, Dr. Close will be there with me through it all, so you have nothing to fear in that respect."

Agatha sighs. "Then you should do it. Your father was a gifted and meticulous neurosurgeon and if he had the confidence to leave his hospital in your care, we trust you completely."

Mayor Wembley nods. "I'm with my wife on this."

"Thanks for believing in me, my team and I will do our best not to let you both down."

I appreciate Saul and Agatha's confidence in me and my abilities, but that doesn't mean my nerves have let up.

So far, my team and I have had eleven practice runs and finished six of them with little to no incident. In my own spare time, I have completed about thirty of them. Still, a craniotomy is one of the most complicated and highest-risk surgeries a neurosurgeon can perform.

No matter how prepared you are in theory, during the actual surgery, a million unanticipated things could go wrong. You need to have nerves of steel for such an adventure and right now my nerves are jelly at best.

I need to go where I can clear my head and do my best thinking—the gym. I grab the set of gym wear that I keep in my office and as I'm heading out, I see Dr. Thorne walking out of a patient's room, her assistant Laura by her side.

"So what did you need?" I ask when she gets to where I'm standing.

She puts her pen into her breast pocket. "Never mind, I figured it out on my own."

I manage to crack a smile. "That's what I love to hear. I'm going to the gym and I'll be back in an hour, but you can reach me on my cell."

"Okay, doc," she says, walking away with Laura who was staring at me intently throughout our exchange.

From the tone of her voice, I can tell she's upset with the way I dismissed her earlier but frankly, her displeasure is the least of my concerns right now.

I go outside, get into my Tesla, and in ten minutes I'm at the gym.

Aiden, my best friend and gym buddy, is already there, so I put on my gear and join him to sweat off my anxiety. Forty minutes later, I feel energized but my mind is still foggy like the skies on a cold day.

"Do you want to talk about it?" Aiden asks as we cool down with some light stretching exercises.

"Talk about what?"

"Whatever's got you looking like someone who just got some bad news."

"It's nothing," I sigh. "I just have a surgery tomorrow that's weighing on my shoulders."

"You mean Priscilla Wembley's surgery?"

I look at him, utterly shocked at what I just heard. "How do you know about her surgery?"

"I think the whole town knows. Mayor Wembley and his wife have been asking people to put Priscilla in their prayers."

I shake my head. "Great, I'm under enough pressure as it is without the whole town counting on me."

"I know you can do it, bud. You didn't graduate from Harvard Medical School and do your residency in one of the best hospitals in the country for nothing. You're a master at your craft."

"Yeah. It's great you and the Wembleys trust me so much, because my dad does not think I can do this surgery." I pause. "What if he's right?"

"For starters, your dad is an ass, so his opinion doesn't count."

"My dad was one of the best neurosurgeons in Texas—his opinion counts more than God's for a lot of people."

"The keyword being *was*. And he's not right. It's your time now, my friend. You've got this. Trust yourself, everyone else does."

"Thanks for saying all that, Aiden." I eye him suspiciously. "You're being overly generous with your compliments today, what do you want?"

"Must I want something before I can say nice things about my friend?"

I laugh. "Not at all."

"Okay, you may be right about me wanting something. You remember my younger sister Lily?"

"I'm not sure. I think the last time I saw her was before I left for medical school, which was twelve years ago."

"Yeah, so she's back to Elvesridge from New York, and you would be doing me a solid if you could find a place for her in your hospital."

I take a sip of my water. "I didn't know your sister was a doctor."

"She's not. She's a physician's assistant and she can help at the hospital."

A physician's assistant is just what I need, but PAs seldom leave the big hospitals in the big cities—especially New York—to come to look for work in Elvesridge unless they're trying to hide or run from something.

"I wish I could help, but right now we don't need physician's assistants," I lie.

"Come on, Lev. She's a hard worker, really brilliant and driven. I'm sure you can squeeze her in somewhere," he says as we head to the changing room.

"Alright, fine. Tell her to come by tomorrow and I'll see what I can do."

A broad smile spreads across Levi's face. "Thanks, man. She will be excited about this."

"You're welcome," I say, stepping into the shower for a quick wash.

Chapter Three

Lilian

I've been sitting in the reception area of Greenwood Hospital for about thirty minutes waiting to see Levi Greenwood.

When Aiden informed me last night that he wanted me to come by the hospital today and see him, I was over the moon and determined to impress him enough to hopefully land the job there and then.

The hospital is a lot bigger than I remember. Being one of the only two hospitals in Elvesridge, most of the town folk, including my own family, come here to get treatment. I see some familiar faces sitting around waiting to be seen by a doctor and I carefully avoid their gazes.

My head is buried in my phone when a lanky-looking guy who couldn't be anything above twenty-one walks up to me.

"Excuse me, Ms. Weatherby, Dr. Greenwood is ready for you. Please come with me."

Picking up my bag, I follow him into the elevator and we ride up to a floor that is very different from the busy general area we've just come from.

"You must be a VIP patient?" The lanky guy asks me as we walk down the long corridor.

"What do you mean?"

"Dr. Greenwood only personally sees very important patients. Except in complicated cases, of course," he adds as if to justify the first part of his sentence.

"I don't think that's information you should be giving to someone who doesn't work here." *Yet.*

"You can go in," he says with a smirk that lets me know he doesn't appreciate my unsolicited advice.

Pushing open the door, I enter the most organized and lush office I've ever been in. There's a cream leather sofa, cream-colored walls, and neatly arranged shelves with so many medical books it would take days to count them all.

"Please have a seat," a man hunched over his desk, writing on a paper, says to me without looking up.

I could swear I've heard that deep velvet-smooth voice before—it's an unforgettable one.

I quickly scan his features.

Sandy-brown hair. Too much hair gel. Broad Thor-like shoulders... He looks up at me. *Blue eyes.*

Oh shit!

"You!" I say, gawking at him like I've seen a ghost. My heart is beating so fast I'm afraid his doctor ears might pick up on it.

"Well, well, if it isn't the first woman to ever call me a psycho besides my mother," he says, scanning me from top to bottom.

Damn, he heard me call him a psycho.

"At least I'm in good company," I say, managing to get some saliva going in my dry mouth.

"If you knew her, you wouldn't say that."

"In my defense, I remember you calling me a moron first."

"After you said you would sue the pants off me."

He has me dead to rights with that and I don't have any comebacks so I stare at him, half expecting him to ask me out of his office.

"So, you're Levi's sister?" he asks, almost as though he's disappointed by that fact.

"Yes, Lilian Weatherby."

He leans back into his swivel chair and stares at me coldly. "He told me you were a physician's assistant in New York. For how long and what hospital were you with?"

"Actually, I just got my PA certification and haven't worked anywhere with it but I'm a fast learner and I've been in many ORs and ERs before now."

He stares at me, his clear-cut blue eyes unwavering from mine, so I ramble on.

"I have all my certifications in this file," I say, handing him a copy of my credentials.

As he goes through them, his face expressionless, I can't tell if he's impressed or if he wants to throw them in the trash beside his desk.

He eventually looks up at me, and for the first time, I notice that the tip of his nose is a little crooked. Still, it takes nothing away from his perfectly structured face.

He presses a bell on his table and a few seconds later the scrawny secretary pops in his head.

"Give these to Dr. Thorne and tell her Ms. Weatherby will be assisting her for the day. That's if you can start work right away," he says, but I don't realize the remark is directed toward me.

I was too busy watching the tiniest movements of his thin red lips as he addressed his secretary to hear him.

"Ms. Weatherby? I asked if you could start working right away."

I scramble to collect my thoughts before responding in a calm voice.

"Of course I can start right away. Thanks for giving me a chance, I won't let you down."

I wait a few seconds for his response, but when none is forthcoming, I take my file and leave his office.

It's my first day at work and going by our little interaction in his office, my boss already hates me. I'm not his biggest fan either. After all, he did almost run me over and he definitely called me a moron.

Of all the two thousand plus men in Elvesridge, the one I called a psycho after clearly being in the wrong just so happens to be my boss. Can you see what I'm saying about being a magnet for bad luck?

As we walk toward the elevator, Levi's secretary comes up with an excuse of having eaten something bad and needing to use the restroom, but I'm sure he just doesn't want to help me.

"Are you Dr. Thorne?" I ask a lady in navy blue scrubs when I get back to the ground floor.

She drags her eyes from one of her patient's files and shoots me an annoyed glance. "What does my name tag say?"

"Dr. Thorne," I reply, feeling foolish.

"Are you gonna keep staring at me or are you gonna tell me why you're looking for me?"

"Dr. Greenwood asked me to give you this."

She takes the paper from my hand and scans through it before shoving it back into my hand.

"I don't have the time or the patience to baby anyone today. I have like a dozen patients to attend to and my PA Laura keeps disappearing on me," she says, looking around for who I assume is Laura.

"I can help you. I may be new, but I'm a quick study."

She eyes me, uncertainty etched into her features. "Don't expect any princess treatment from me or anyone here just because you're a Weatherby."

"I didn't think—"

"Good. You're not here to think, you're here to do what I tell you. And make sure you're not wearing these the next time I see you," she says before stepping into a patient's room.

She means the navy blue pants and long-sleeved chiffon shirt I wore for my interview. From my encounter with Dr. Thorne, I have no doubt the next few hours will be a thorn in my flesh.

As I look around, wondering where I can grab a fresh pair of scrubs, the elevator opens and I see a young girl who from all indications is Priscilla Wembley. She's being wheeled out of the elevator, her parents walking beside her.

Her surgery has been the talk of the town for days now and I heard Levi is performing it himself. Maybe that's why he was wound up when I met with him.

Yeah, that or simply because he hates my guts.

I watch as Priscilla's parents get to the doors where they aren't allowed to go past. The raw emotions on their faces as they say what I hope are their temporary goodbyes to their daughter bring a sting to my eye.

After she's wheeled in, a nurse leads them to the waiting room for what I'm certain will be the longest wait of their lives.

I'm about to go find my scrubs when I hear a loud screech outside followed by the hospital doors suddenly bursting open. Some paramedics rush in with a young man on a stretcher, a blood-soaked cloth on his abdomen, blood oozing from his side, and his face contorted with pain.

"We need a doctor now!" one of the paramedics yells.

Dr. Thorne runs out of the patient's room she'd been in, hurriedly puts on some gloves, and rushes over to the patient on the stretcher.

"His name is Jason Bennett, eighteen years old. He and two other bikers were involved in a mountain biking accident but his case is the most critical as one of the bicycle handles is lodged in his abdomen," the older of the two paramedics briefs her.

"Hello, Jason. Can you hear me? You're at Greenwood Hospital and we're going to take good care of you," Dr. Thorne says, raising the blood-soaked towel.

I gasp when I see the bicycle handle sticking out of his abdomen.

As the doctor and nurses battle with Jason, the door bursts open again and this time, two sets of paramedics carry in two young boys who I assume are the other bikers.

Another doctor and nurse take charge of one of the boys—he's bleeding from a head injury and has lost consciousness—while Dr. Thorne calls for another doctor to take on the third patient, Carl.

While they're still trying to figure out who can handle Carl, he stops breathing.

My training kicks in, and I slip on a pair of gloves. With the help of the paramedics, we transfer Carl to an empty bed, and I begin administering CPR before the paramedics get another emergency call and leave us to our fate.

Shortly after Carl comes to, I notice that he's breathing faster than usual, and his chest has unusual movement patterns.

"I think he's in respiratory distress," I call out to Dr. Thorne.

I hear her tell the nurse applying pressure on Jason to do an intubation on my patient.

"But I've never done it before," she protests.

"You've watched me do it countless times, I know you can do it. And I'll talk you through it."

"We're running out of time, he's turning blue," I call out again and the nurse rushes over to me with the intubation kit.

"You." Dr. Thorne signals to me. "Come help me apply pressure to Jason's abdomen."

"You good?" I ask the nurse, she nods in agreement and right after my CPR cycle ends, she takes over the chest compression, so I run over to Jason.

"The X-ray shows that the bicycle handle didn't hit any major organs but it's pressing against the liver and may puncture it if we don't act fast. I have to get it out now."

"What do you need me to do?"

"When I pull it out, there'll be a lot of blood so I'll need you to apply pressure to help control the bleeding."

I nod, and she proceeds to do a countdown. "Three, two, one, now!"

In a panic, I press on an artery, and the patient's blood splatters all over me before I can get the clean cloth over the open area.

"Did any get in your mouth?" she asks me and I nod yes, tasting the blood in my mouth.

"Shit! How are we doing, Lucy?" she asks and I look over at the nurse to see her hand shaking profusely.

"I don't think I can do this," she replies, her voice a little shaky.

Dr. Thorne turns to me. "Have you ever done an intubation before?"

I nod in the affirmative, a million things running through my mind.

What if this man has Hepatitis B or syphilis or worse still HIV? I could be infected for life.

I've never really thought about swallowing my saliva before, but right now it's taking all I have not to swallow it.

"Can you do it now?"

I nod again.

"Then go!"

Running over to Carl, I grab the intubation kit from the nurse who is frozen in place by now.

"Lucy, come over here," Dr. Thorne calls to the nurse and she leaves my side.

As my heart thumps wildly against my chest, I position Carl in such a way that his neck is slightly extended, then I introduce an oxygen device to oxygenate his lungs and make sure he has enough oxygen reserves before I proceed.

After lubricating the endotracheal tube, I insert the laryngoscope blade to get a clear view of his throat.

Once that's done, I take a deep breath before inserting the ET tube through the vocal cords and into the trachea, not stopping until I hear Carl let out a deep breath, his chest rising and falling in a normal rhythm.

I heave a sigh of relief and secure the tube in place with tape.

The other male doctor and nurse are still battling with the second patient, Jimmy, when I run off to rinse my mouth with some mouth-wash.

When I return from the bathroom, Jason is now in minimal pain and Dr. Thorne is helping the male doctor stabilize Jimmy.

With all three patients out of the danger zone and being closely monitored, Dr. Thorne comes to stand beside me at the foot of Jason's bed.

"We've taken his blood to the lab and in a few minutes we'll have the test results back."

I nod, too nervous to speak.

She smiles at me reassuringly, her white teeth matching her bleached blonde hair packed into a ponytail.

"Welcome to the ER, Lilian Weatherby."

As I see the lab technician walking toward us, a vague look on his face, my heart starts pounding again, my forehead breaking into a cold sweat.

"I found no traces of Hepatitis B, C, HIV, or any other disease in the blood sample. It's clean."

"Oh, thank God," I say, letting out my breath which I didn't know I was holding in.

Dr. Thorne pats me gently on the back before walking away.

This has got to be the most chaotic first day in the history of first days, I think to myself, looking at my chiffon shirt ruined with blood stains.

I need to get out of these clothes and I need a drink. Or three.

Chapter Four

♥

Levi

As I step out of the OR after Priscilla Wembley's surgery, my heart swells with pride. A procedure that I had believed would take at least four to five hours was completed in three.

Even though I accidentally nicked a blood vessel and her blood pressure dropped lower than normal a few times, we managed to rectify those issues and finish the surgery with no other major complications.

As I walk into the waiting room post-surgery, the mayor and his wife all but run toward me and I flash them a reassuring smile.

"How did it go, doc? How is Priscilla?"

"Everything went marvelously well. I was able to take out all the blood clots in the brain and the swelling has reduced significantly. Now we wait for Priscilla to wake up, which I know she will. She's a fighter."

The Wembleys hug each other and then they both hug me. "Thank you so much for giving our daughter a second chance to live."

"It's my absolute pleasure. Although we're not yet out of the woods, I'm confident she'll wake up and make a full recovery."

"Can we see her now?"

"Sure. She's currently in the ICU so you can only stay with her for an hour."

"Thank you once again, Dr. Greenwood," Agatha Wembley says, taking my hand in hers.

"You're welcome, Agatha."

As I walk away, beaming with smiles, I'm reminded of why I became a neurosurgeon—to put a smile on the faces of families who would've otherwise lost hope.

Typically after surgeries like these, I'm always tired and have to head home to rest. Today, I feel deliciously alive.

Not to get too cocky yet, but *suck it, Dad, you said I wouldn't be able to do it and yet here I am.*

Changing into my T-shirt and jeans, I throw on a leather jacket and go in search of Dr. Thorne.

"Whoa, what the hell happened here?" I ask her when I see the ER in disarray.

"Mountain biking accidents, things lodged in places they shouldn't be, you know, the usual."

I look around and see Aiden's sister standing at a patient's bed, looking at their chart, the curves I've seen on her hidden underneath blue scrubs.

"Was the newbie here when all this chaos went down?"

"Yes she was, and she held her own despite it being a very challenging first day for her. Save for a little blood spatter scare which turned out to be nothing, she impressed me."

Dr. Thorne isn't one to throw around compliments, which means Lilian truly impressed her. I'm eager to know more about the blood spatter scare Dr. Thorne referred to, but I'd rather she not think I have any special interest in Lilian.

"I heard the surgery went well," she continues.

"It did. That's actually why I'm here. I want you to personally keep an eye on the Wembley girl till she wakes up, which I believe will be in the next few hours."

"You got it, doc."

At that moment, Lilian looks up at me. Our eyes meet and I quickly avert my gaze and head for my car.

The Rusty Rail is alive with activity when I walk in. Drunk men are chattering loudly while couples sway to the music of the singer on stage. I walk up to the bar area and ask the bartender Mitch for a shot of whiskey.

After downing the shot, I wait for the singer on stage to finish her performance so I can take the stage. As soon as she's done, I get on, and a few minutes into my performance I see my worst nightmare walk in, wearing a sleeveless top and a short leather skirt.

What the hell is she doing this far out of town, in my favorite bar?

For months I've been coming to sing at the Rusty Rail because folk from Elvesridge hardly come here. Until tonight. 'Cause Lilian Weatherby is staring right at me.

I continue singing, trying hard to not let the tension I'm feeling break through my voice. I watch from the corner of my eye as she goes to the bar, orders a drink, and turns around to watch the rest of my performance.

Managing to get through it without mumbling like an idiot, the thought of pretending not to have seen her crosses my mind—but it's pointless since the bar is only so big.

"Wow, those are some powerful chords you got there," she says as I sit beside her at the bar.

"You can drop the act. I'm not your boss outside the hospital."

"What act? I'm being serious. You're really good."

I turn to look at her and I'm temporarily taken aback by her beauty.

The few times I've seen her she's had her hair in a ponytail, but now her wavy blonde hair with dark roots frames her shapely oval face. Light brown eyes stare at me through long brown lashes and I can't help but notice her rosy red lips.

Her breasts, which seem a little big for her small frame, peek at me through her semi-see-through blouse.

Supple breasts are my Achilles heel and Lilian's look voluptuous. I can't stop my mind from drifting, imagining what touching them, sucking on them, would feel like.

Dammit, she's Aiden's sister and my employee. I shouldn't be thinking about her breasts.

"Considering how deep your voice is, I never would've guessed you could sing, let alone hit a B4."

"B4?" I ask, clearing my throat, now husky from my lustful thoughts. "Only someone who knows music would know what precise notes I sing."

I catch a glimpse of sadness in her eyes before she looks away. "I've been singing since I was eight years old. Thought I'd become a singer one day, but life had other plans."

That doesn't explain the sadness I caught in her eyes, but I deduce she doesn't want me to probe any further so I change the subject.

"So who's your favorite band?"

She flashes me a wry smile. "I know this may seem weird, but hear me out. It's The Flaming Lips."

"Really?" I ask, narrowing my eyes suspiciously.

"What? You think I'm too young to love The Flaming lips?" she asks, tilting her head to the side.

I catch a scar on her eyebrow from the reflection of the bar lights. The sudden urge to trace the scar with my fingers hits me but I refrain myself.

"I didn't say that. Favorite song?"

"That's easy, 'Sun Blows Up Today' from their 2013 album, *The Terror*."

I throw my hands up. "Alright, I believe you, you are a Lipper."

"I was devastated when Michael Ivan left," we say in unison, our eyes fixated on each other with mutual admiration.

I'm sure I'm making her uncomfortable with my staring, but I can't seem to peel my eyes away from hers.

Maybe it's the dim lights of the bar, or the soft music playing in the background, or simply the fact that I find her so irresistible, but I'm suddenly overwhelmed with the need to kiss her.

Yes, it's a need, just like I need my next breath.

My eyes drop to her plump lips and when she bites on the lower one, I take that as an invitation and lean in for a kiss hoping to God I didn't misread the situation.

When she brings her face closer to mine, her eyes fluttering closed, the noise all around us fades away as I take her full lips into mine.

Her lips, generous, warm, and inviting, are softer than I imagined. Her scent, a captivating blend of floral and fruity notes, wafts into my nostrils.

The sweetness of the vodka she was drinking earlier still lingers in her mouth, driving me to want more, to taste more of her.

Her skin, soft against my face, feels like fine silk. I deepen the kiss, my tongue slipping into her mouth to find hers ready to mingle.

My hands seem to develop a mind of their own as they weave through her soft hair, drop down to her neck, and make their way to the small of her back.

She sucks in a deep breath and my hands freeze. Afraid that I've crossed a line, I break the kiss and stare at her face which is flushed from the passionate meeting of our lips.

"Wow, that was…" She trails off.

"Yeah, it was…" I reply, and we both let out an awkward laugh.

***

I can't believe I kissed Lilian Weatherby.

Being professional and never getting involved with anyone who works in my hospital is one thing I've always prided myself on until she came along, soft lips and brown eyes melting away that resolve faster than butter over heat.

As I step into the hospital, I look around, releasing my breath when I don't see her anywhere in sight. The last thing I need right now is to run into her so soon after our decadent kiss. A kiss after which I made up a silly excuse and disappeared due to my guilt.

I dash for the elevator, get inside, and press the button for the third floor. The elevator stops at the first floor and who do you think is standing there when it slides open? Lilian, the one person I didn't want to see.

"Hi, Ms. Weatherby," I say casually as though we were not exchanging bodily fluids just last night.

"Hi, Dr. Greenwood. I hope no sirens were called to your house last night."

"What?" I ask, stealing a glance in her direction.

"Last night. You said you needed to go make sure you didn't leave your stove on."

This is ridiculous. I convinced my attending to allow me to go solo in a peripheral nerve surgery in my second year of residency but I couldn't come up with a better excuse than "I left my stove on"?

"Turns out I didn't leave it on."

"Happens to me all the time too."

I can clearly hear the sarcasm in her voice.

"So I've assigned you to assist Dr. Thorne and the ER department till further notice so you won't need to keep coming upstairs."

The elevator doors open and I step out so fast one would think I was hurrying to leave a bloody crime scene.

Deciding to do my rounds right away, I start with Priscilla Wembley's room. I am very pleased to find her awake and her parents grinning from ear to ear.

"You'll have to take it easy for a few days, but you should be able to go home by the weekend."

"Thank you, Dr. Greenwood."

"You're welcome, Priscilla."

My next patient is Sheriff Adams' wife who was admitted with severe stomach pain. I go through her chart and see that the results of the test I sent her to carry out are not yet in her folder on my iPad.

"Why are her test results not yet here?" I ask Phil, my nurse who's doing the rounds with me.

"Last time I asked, the lab said they weren't done with it."

"What? Seems like anything I want done I'll have to do myself."

Leaving the room, I decide to go down to the lab myself and get those results if I have to.

Turns out it was a bad decision because as I get to the lab, I see Lilian there and none of the lab guys are in sight.

We stare at each other awkwardly for a few moments and I wish I had sent Phil down here instead.

"Where is everyone?"

"They went to get some supplies from the pharmacy."

"I see," I reply, scratching the back of my neck.

"Okay then," she says, deciding to leave at the exact moment I decide to check and see if the lab is locked and we almost collide into each other.

As we stand there, staring at each other, electricity crackling between us, one of the lab guys whose presence we hadn't noticed clears his throat, forcing us to come apart.

Chapter Five

♥

Lilian

With all the awkwardness between Levi and me at the hospital, the last thing I need is more awkwardness at home. However, my parents have insisted on throwing a dinner party to celebrate my return, and awkward conversations are always on the menu of any gathering involving all my family members.

"So I hear you're working at Greenwood Hospital as a physician's assistant?" Aunt Florence asks after we say grace.

"That's right," I respond, trying to cut a piece of my steak into two.

"Isn't that the hospital now run by William Greenwood's handsome son Levi?"

"Yes, it is," Aiden offers.

"Isn't he older than you?" she asks Aiden, and he agrees with a nod. "Which means he should be looking to get married by now." She turns her attention back to me. "You need to get him to notice you, maybe you'll finally get a ring on that finger of yours."

"I'm not looking to get into any relationship right now," I say, trying very hard not to sound as irritated as I feel.

"When I was your age, I was already married with two kids."

"That's enough, Florence. Lily is young, she still has plenty of time to get married."

I stare at my mom, surprised that she's speaking up for me.

"What she needs now is to figure out what she wants to do with her life. She's wasted nine years already in New York and God knows how much she'll waste being a physician's assistant instead of an actual physician. Last I checked you majored in neurosurgery didn't you?"

Of course there's a catch. There's always a catch with my mom.

"Both of you, stop it. This is a family dinner, not an FBI interrogation."

I love my dad but I don't need him fighting this battle for me.

"Mom, I'd rather *waste* ten more years as a physician's assistant than one working with you, and Aunt Flo—didn't your husband find out your second child wasn't his and leave you?"

The whole table falls silent, Aunt Florence's round face looking a lot rounder with her jaw wide open. The only noise in the room is that of my knife scraping against my plate as I cut my steak, beaming at the aftermath of my savagery.

"Did you ever see Paul in New York after I left?" Aunt Betty asks, breaking the silence.

"Why are you still so hung up on Paul? You were the one who asked him for a divorce, remember?" Aunt Jane—Dad's sister—asks Aunt Betty.

She glares angrily at Aunt Jane. "I'm not hung up on him, I just asked a simple question."

"Yeah, I did see him once. With his wife and baby."

"What wife and baby? We aren't even legally divorced yet." From Aunt Betty's expression, it's clear she didn't have a clue that Paul remarried or that he had a baby.

Aunt Jane scoffs. "If you're not still hung up on him, why are you so bothered then?"

"I'm so sorry, Aunt Betty. I thought you knew."

I truly thought she knew about Paul. I wouldn't intentionally want to hurt her, because she's the only one at this table apart from Aiden and my dad who has not gotten on my last nerve since I got home.

Unfortunately, she doesn't stay in the Weatherby mansion with the rest of us, which tips the scale in favor of those who annoy me.

My grandparents aren't bad either, but they're out on a date right now, which is amazing in itself.

"That's enough talking from everyone, let's eat dinner in peace, please," Dad says. Everyone is happy to oblige, including my mom who doesn't say another word until dinner is over.

We spend the rest of the dinner in silence except for the occasional "pass the salt and pepper" interruptions.

After dinner, Dad comes into my room to speak with me.

"Honey, I don't like how harsh you were with your mom at dinner. She loves you and only wants the best for you. You don't know how difficult your leaving was for both of us, but especially for her. Please cut her some slack, okay?"

"Alright, fine. I'll try, but make sure you tell her to stop getting on my nerves too."

"Deal," Dad says, looking like he still has something weighing on him. "So, what really happened in New York? Why are you a physician's assistant?"

"I don't think I'm ready to talk about it."

"It's okay, I'll be here whenever you're ready to talk."

"Thanks, Dad."

"And one more thing," he says, getting up. "Don't tell your mom I spoke to you about this."

"Your secret is safe with me," I say, running my hand over my lips as though I'm closing a zipper.

***

The next morning when I get to work by seven, Dr. Thorne is already there so I knock softly on the door of her office.

"Come on in."

Her office is very different from Levi's. There are patient files strewn everywhere on her desk; the phone is barely visible underneath.

On the wall behind her, there's a pediatric cardiology degree from Harvard with her full name, *Teresa Thorne*, written on it, alongside many other awards.

She doesn't look like a Teresa. All the Teresas I know are bigger in stature, while Dr. Thorne and I are almost the same height.

There's a book about irregular heartbeats half opened in front of her and she's flipping through a file which she hands to me. From my observation, she's one of the few doctors in the hospital who still uses physical files for patients instead of iPads.

"Patient A, Brian Davis, nine years old, was admitted yesterday with an irregular heartbeat, extreme fatigue, dizziness, chest pain, and difficulty breathing."

I study the file in my hand intently. "Has there been any fainting?"

"Not since he was admitted. So, what do you think his diagnosis is?"

"From what I have here in his chart, his heart rate is in the mid-60s instead of 70-110. Coupled with the other symptoms, I would have to say the patient has symptomatic bradycardia."

"And what treatment course would you recommend?"

"A pacemaker implantation is necessary if the bradycardia is persistent and non-responsive to other treatments like placing him on Atropine."

Dr. Thorne isn't big on expressions, so I have to rely on a slight nod of her head to know she's impressed with my diagnosis and treatment plan.

She hands me another patient file. "Patient 2, Brian O'Connor, thirty-four years old, showed signs of dizziness, fatigue, chest pain, difficulty breathing, headaches, and vision loss. What would you say is his diagnosis?"

"It says here that his blood pressure is 202 over 110. Combined with his symptoms he has severe hypertension."

"And what is the best treatment plan for him?"

"Beta-blockers and Lisinopril will do the trick, coupled with lifestyle changes."

"Good. Come with me and let's go see our patients," she says, grabbing her stethoscope.

I'm surprised because I genuinely thought the patients were made up due to their similar names and symptoms.

When we get to Brian Davis' room, she places the stethoscope on his chest to listen to his heartbeat.

"It's quite low, get me some Atropine from his cart."

"There's none here," I say after thoroughly searching the cart.

"Alright, get some from the nurse's station."

When I search the nurse's station, there's no Atropine there either so she tells me to go and grab some from the central supply room.

I head for the central supply room where all the drugs are kept in bulk and just as I'm about to go in, I hear my name being mentioned so I stop to eavesdrop.

"I don't understand why she got a job so quickly. I've been telling Dr. Greenwood about my younger brother who needs a job for months now and he keeps telling me there's no room for new hires, yet as soon as she comes along, he makes room."

"Maybe he has the hots for her," the second nurse suggests.

"No way, she's hardly his type. Dr. Levi loves super hot blondes, she's just blonde."

"And not even the good type of blonde, she has dark roots." They both laugh.

"I'm sure she got the job because of her last name. I heard Dr. Greenwood and that hot brother of hers are best friends," the first nurse says.

"But I heard she did well in the ER the other day."

"Probably beginner's luck. Let's see the entitled brat last for more than a month."

At this point, I can't take it anymore.

"If I were an entitled brat like you say, it wouldn't make sense for me to be working here, would it? I would be off vacationing on an island somewhere or I'd be in Africa pretending to help dig wells and posting about it all over social media for applause," I say, taking the two of them by surprise.

They stare at me, tongue-tied.

"Why the silence? Don't you have any more witty comments to make? I see the cat got your tongues, huh."

They remain silent and then hurriedly exit the room.

Could my first week at Greenwood Hospital get any worse?

First, my boss hates me, then we shared one of the best kisses I've ever had, and now he's doing everything humanly possible to avoid me like a plague when I haven't been able to stop thinking about our kiss.

My mom, for her part, thinks I'm wasting my time here. Now I'm finding out many of the nurses dislike me for no reason other than my last name, which I'm not even milking the way other members of my family do.

I gather the supplies and quickly head back to Dr. Thorne but I run into her hurrying down the hall.

"There's an emergency in room 105 that needs my attention. Please give Brian his injections and wait till I get back to visit our other patient."

"Yes, doctor."

As I put some of the medications into the nurse's station, I happen to look up and I see Levi—who I assume was on call all night—stepping out of the elevator. A blonde, the type that the nurses in the supply room just described, is walking beside him arm in arm.

She whispers something to him and he laughs as they make their way toward the hospital's entrance.

Watching them feels like someone turned up the temperature to a thousand degrees.

God! I can't believe I've been thinking about our kiss while he's been out kissing or doing worse with other women.

How could I be so foolish to think that an eligible bachelor like Levi liked me enough to send other women away—women who offered themselves up on a platter—just because we kissed at a bar? He's probably kissed many other women at that same bar.

He doesn't even look in my direction, he just walks straight out the door and I don't see him anymore.

My chest feels tight with anger. Part of me feels like going to confront him while the other part feels like quitting here and now, but I do neither. I just flip through Brian's file, grab his injections, and go to his room.

"Hi Brian, how are you feeling?" I ask the bright-eyed young boy.

"I'm feeling okay."

"My name is Lilian and I'm here to administer your routine medications to you."

"Will there be any shots?"

"Not from me. Are you scared of needles?"

"Yeah, a little bit, and my friends always tease me for that."

"Can I tell you a secret?" He nods enthusiastically. "I used to be scared of needles too when I was your age."

"Really? How did you stop getting scared then?"

"Who says I stopped? I'm still scared of needles but the fear is less when I think about how the shots will help me heal. You want to go home and play with your friends again right?"

"Yes."

"These medications will help make sure of that, so think about that next time okay?"

While Brian and I are still talking, I put the required dosage of his injection into the syringe, go to his drip stand, and inject the liquid into his drip bag just as it's written in his file.

Not more than fifteen seconds after I administer the drug, Brian's vital signs machine begins beeping furiously and he loses consciousness.

I press the emergency code button and start CPR before Dr. Thorne runs into the room. "What happened?"

"I gave him an atenolol."

"What? That's a beta blocker. Quick, grab an epinephrine from the nurse's station," she says, stopping the drip from getting into his system.

I remain rooted on the spot, heart pounding, hands stone-cold, sweat pouring down my face.

"Lilian, now!" she yells, snapping me out of my temporary paralysis.

I grab an epinephrine from the nurse's station and race back to Brian's room where an oxygen mask has been put on his face.

Brian's mom tries to come into the room but some nurses stop her and lead her away from the scene.

My hands shaking profusely, I hand Dr. Thorne the epinephrine and she quickly jams a shot of it into his thigh.

I watch in horror as the beeping from the vital signs machine slows down and his blood pressure and pulse gradually comes back up.

"How the hell did this happen?" Dr. Thorne asks when we leave Brian's room.

"I...I...I don't know. I just gave him the injection that was written down in his chart."

"I treated him and there's no way in hell I could've added a beta blocker to the list of medications a bradycardia patient would take."

By now, the attention of everyone on the ground floor of the hospital is on us.

"Show me his file."

Still shaking, I hand her the first file on the desk, and in one glance, she sees my error.

I interchanged the two Brians' medications because I was distracted by Levi and his bimbo.

"Do you know what could've happened if I hadn't acted fast? That little boy could've died. Go home! Get out of here and don't come back till you have your head on straight."

Grabbing my purse, I run out of the hospital, and once I'm outside, I throw up.

Chapter Six

♥

Levi

"Levi!" I hear my dad yell from his room.

I open my eyes and glance at my phone—which is charging on my nightstand—to see that it's a few minutes past nine which means I barely got an hour of sleep after my hectic night at the hospital.

"Levi!" he calls again, and I swear into my pillow.

I throw on a pair of brown shorts over the briefs I was wearing when I collapsed into bed and head over to Dad's room. I find him sitting up on his bed, a frustrated look plastered across his face.

There's a round wet stain where he's sitting and he rushes to explain when he sees me looking at it.

"I tried to get up to use the bathroom but these damn stiff joints wouldn't let me."

I put my arms underneath his armpits and pull him up out of the wet stain and into a cane chair beside the bed.

"This won't happen if you allow me to keep a bedpan beside you."

"I don't need a fucking bedpan, I'm not an invalid."

"Fine," I say, rumpling up the soiled bedsheet and taking it to the laundry room.

When I come back to Dad's room, I help him out of his wet pajamas and into some dry clothes before I proceed to massage and give his joints some light stretching.

Things aren't always this bad. Some days he wakes up strong and jolly—well, not jolly. I don't think I've ever seen my dad jolly, not even before he was diagnosed with rheumatoid arthritis a year and a half ago.

In his usual stubborn manner, he ignored the diagnosis and continued working at the hospital until one day he tried getting up and couldn't, and his secretary had to help him. His doctor told him that if he didn't take his diagnosis seriously, his joints would give up on him and he would be permanently deformed.

Since RA affects the joints of the fingers and wrists, he was forced to stop operating on patients. I've never seen my dad cry, not even when Mom died, but I swear he shed some tears when he found out he would never be in the OR again.

"I'm okay now," he says ten minutes into the massage, but I ignore him and continue stretching his arms.

Just like me, needing help makes Dad feel uncomfortable and slightly emasculated, but that doesn't change the fact that he needs it.

A licensed physiotherapist or masseur should be doing this, but the three I hired so far didn't last a week due to Dad's terrible attitude and grumpiness toward them. I don't blame them, I'd have quit a long time ago if he wasn't my dad.

Dad has always been a difficult man to please or impress. Even as a kid I found myself constantly yearning for his approval. I often studied till my eyes were bloodshot to make sure I always came out on top of my class, I had no friends except for Aiden who stuck around no matter how many times I tried to get rid of him, my social life was nonexistent, and I didn't have a girlfriend till I was in my third year of med school.

I was so desperate to please my dad that I became a neurosurgeon just like him. And what did I get after graduating from Harvard Medical School as the best in my class? A pat on the back from Mr. Grumpy himself.

Even now, as a thirty-eight-year-old man, the man still keeps me on my tippy toes. It fucking sucks, believe me.

"How's the hospital?"

"Fine."

"Any interesting new cases?"

"Nope."

"I'm surprised the mayor went ahead to allow you to do his daughter's craniotomy."

I raise my brows suspiciously. "What do you mean *went ahead*?"

"I advised him against it," Dad responds coolly.

I could honestly knock my dad out right now and not think twice about it, but I know he's deliberately trying to get a rise out of me. Why else would he bring up the surgery when he knows it was successful if not to provoke me?

"Good thing he didn't listen to you. You got it from here, right?"

"Right."

Thanks for your help, son.

You're welcome, Dad.

Yeah, that conversation wouldn't even happen in my dreams. Maybe in an alternate universe where my dad isn't an unfeeling robot.

"By the way, I'll be stopping by the hospital tomorrow," he says, just as I'm about to leave the room. "I wanna come see how much you've run it into the ground."

I turn to face him. "Suit yourself, it's still your hospital after all," I say in such a calm tone that no one would ever guess my heart is racing like I've just run a marathon.

***

One hour later, I pull into my reserved parking spot at the hospital. After Dad informed me about his visit, I couldn't go back to sleep. I tossed and turned and eventually decided that coming back to the hospital would be my best bet.

Grabbing the cup of coffee I got from The Sunshine Café on my way here, I step out of the car to see Lilian standing beside the sunflowers.

She's wearing her blue scrubs yet I can see the contours of her gorgeous breasts stretching against the fabric.

Her face looks redder than usual. Confirming my suspicion, she wipes at her eyes with the back of her hands.

Aww hell, there's no way I can throw her a casual hey and escape to my office now. I can't possibly ignore a crying woman, especially not one who is my best friend's sister and the subject of my sensual—not so PG—dreams since our kiss at the bar.

I grab my suitcase and brace myself for what I'm sure will be an awkward exchange. She quickly wipes her eyes and straightens her shoulders when she sees me walking toward her.

"What's wrong?"

"Nothing you should concern yourself with," she responds, her voice a little lower than usual.

"Seeing as you work for me and you're actively weeping in front of my hospital, I'm obligated to make it my concern."

Obligated? Wow, I sound like a douchebag.

Since I met Lilian Weatherby, I've seen her experience anger, lust, passion, and even joy, but I've never seen her afraid...until now.

She sniffles. "I messed up a patient's medication really badly and he almost coded."

Almost is good. "So the patient is still alive?" She nods yes. "I expect you to come inside and be ready to keep doing your job then."

"Dr. Thorne asked me to go home."

"This is my hospital. I get to decide who goes home and who stays, not Dr. Thorne. Come with me."

We walk back into the hospital and head straight to Dr. Thorne's office.

"What is she still doing here?" she asks, looking up at me over the rim of her glasses.

"I told her to come back."

"After what she did? I'm starting to believe the rumors going around."

I'm tempted to ask her what rumors, but I don't have time for hospital gossip. "If we send home everyone who makes a mistake, there'll be no one here half the time. Besides, we've all made our fair share of mistakes."

She takes off her glasses and places them on her desk. "Stella Davis, the patient's mother, has threatened to sue the hospital for negligence."

"I'll handle Mrs. Davis, but right now I have bigger fish to fry."

"What could be bigger than a patient's mother suing us for negligence?"

"My father, visiting the hospital tomorrow."

I watch the blood momentarily drain from her face.

Good, we're now on the same emotional page.

"She can stay, but not as my assistant. Laura may be *friendly* toward the patients, but she's never given any patient the wrong injection."

"Fine," I reply, turning to Lilian who is cowering beside me. "Let's go, we have work to do."

By the end of the evening shift, I call all the hospital staff—medical, nursing, and auxiliary—into the conference room for a brief meeting.

With everyone present, I begin.

"First of all, I'd like to address the whispers that this meeting is about giving everyone a raise, it's not."

I allow them a minute to bemoan the loss of their imaginary raise before I continue.

"The reason I called you all here is to inform you that Dr. William Greenwood, my father, will be visiting the hospital tomorrow. Some of you worked under him, some of you didn't," I say, looking at Lilian. "Those of you who did know what a hard-ass he is, so I need all hands on deck to get this hospital up to William Greenwood standard before tomorrow morning, which means no one is going home until everything is in order."

A ruckus breaks out in the conference room with everyone trying to talk over one another and I'm forced to slap my hand on the desk to call them back to order.

"Janet, I need this place sparkling clean from top to bottom, so see to that. Jolie, I want all the file cabinets to be arranged and every patient's record up-to-date on the system."

"I'm sorry, Dr. Greenwood, but I worked a double shift today and I'm just about ready to shut down for the next eight hours. I don't think I can handle arranging file cabinets."

I squint my eyes at her. "I've gotten approximately two hours of sleep since yesterday yet I'm still standing. You have no excuse," I snap at her before turning my attention to the doctors. "I need every doctor here to go over the case files they've handled this month and correct any mistakes they may have made. And please, for the love of God, put your offices in order."

Dr. Turner, who's been shooting eye daggers at me since I started talking, finally speaks up. "And who will be taking care of our patients while we slave away?"

"Ms. Weatherby and I have got your patients covered." I watch as Lilian's eyes widen in shock over my declaration. "Yes, I know there are over twenty patients but we all have to make sacrifices, right?" I say, more for her benefit than his.

I snap my fingers at Lilian to follow me, and when I see that no one is moving to do the jobs I just assigned to them, I put my head back in the conference room and yell "Now!" which has everyone scrambling to their feet.

Chapter Seven

♥

Lilian

Having spent the remainder of yesterday tasked with assisting Levi to care for about twenty patients, my whole body and soul—if that's possible—hurts, and yet here I am at the crack of dawn on Levi's instructions.

Thank heavens Dad is loaning me his old brown Ford Thunderbird, a car that is very precious to him, to drive while I'm here. I'm certain Aiden wouldn't have appreciated me waking him up at 5:30 in the morning to drive me to the hospital.

Dr. William Greenwood is set to arrive shortly so everyone, notwithstanding how tired they are, is on their feet trying to put things in place.

According to the stories I've heard from the staff that worked with Dr. William, he's a no-nonsense, strict, and arrogant neurosurgeon—*aren't they all*—who ruled the hospital with an iron fist.

"You think Levi is difficult? You should've seen Dr. William rip into us when we messed up," Laura, *the only person in the hospital who seems to like me*, says as we arrange the supply closet.

"Surely it wasn't that bad."

"Oh, it was. No day went by without him making at least one person cry in the OR or the broom closet. One of his nurses even quit in the middle of a surgery one time."

It's hard to believe that the same Dr. William, who was always so sweet to me as a kid, is the same person Laura is talking about.

A loud noise outside attracts our attention. Upon stepping out of the supply room, I see Levi scolding one of the nurses at the nurse's station.

"What do you mean Matthew Miller hasn't been discharged? I sent down all his paperwork before I went home last night. What manner of incompetence is this? Is this how you're going to act when my father gets here? And take a look around you. Why are there files scattered all over the place?"

"We disarranged it searching for Matthew's file," the nurse replies in a squeaky voice.

"Why are you searching for a file? I treated Matthew, not Dr. Thorne, so his chart should be in the system. I would think you'd use that tiny brain of yours for once."

"The systems are down so I couldn't access his charts."

Levi looks like he wants to punch a hole through a wall. "How can the systems be down again? That's what, two times in one week? Fix it."

"I can't."

"Then you are of no use to me."

"You know what?" the nurse says, grabbing her backpack. "I can't do this anymore, I quit!"

Levi watches her leave before turning back to the rest of us. "If anyone else feels like quitting too, the doors are wide open."

Silence. "Get back to work then. Ms. Weatherby, come with me," he says, storming off to his office.

"Good luck," Laura murmurs as I follow Levi, heart in my mouth.

"My father is here," he says as we almost collide near the doorway of his office.

"Yay!" I reply in mock celebration. He shoots me a disgruntled look.

"My secretary, Sam, chose today of all days to call in sick, so I need you to be my assistant and my secretary. Can you handle it?"

His tone tells me that he doesn't mean that as a question.

"Sure, I can."

"Good. I don't need another mumbling idiot by my side today." He presses the elevator button and in no time we're on the ground floor, heading outside to usher in Dr. William.

As Dr. William steps out of his car and walks toward us with a slight limp, I can't help but notice that Levi is the spitting image of him.

Sandy brown hair, that intimidating height, piercing blue eyes. Yup, just like staring twenty years into the future.

"Hi, Dr. Greenwood," I say, stretching out my hand for a handshake which he completely ignores.

Undeterred by his rudeness, I continue. "I don't know if you remember me. I'm Lilian Weatherby, you used to treat me as a kid and I'm honored to be working in your hospital, which is undoubtedly one of the best in the state."

He rests his deep ocean-blue eyes, full of scrutiny on me.

"Aren't you the physician's assistant who got the charts wrong and almost killed a patient? Maybe you should spend less time on flattery and more time learning how to do your job. I would have fired you immediately but apparently, my son is spineless."

I turn to Levi but he looks as shocked as I am at his father's revelation. *Or maybe he's just being a good actor.*

"Am I here for a meet and greet or are we going to get started on what I came for?"

"Of course. After you," Levi says as we walk into the hospital.

Dr. William stops suddenly and my heart just about stops with him. "Is that mold I see on that wall over there?" he says, pointing at some black substance on the wall.

"Yes, the mold removal specialists were supposed to come in yesterday but they rescheduled at the last minute."

Dr. William arches his brows to show that he doesn't believe a word his son is saying. "How about the cleaners, did they reschedule too?" he asks as we walk into reception.

What the heck is this guy's problem? Everywhere is so clean I could eat off the floor.

The atmosphere inside the four walls of the hospital is tense, and everyone seems to be holding their breath as Dr. William walks past them. It's as though he's an inspector from the Health Department whose visit will determine if our doors will stay open or if we'll be shut down.

Dr. Close approaches us and for the first time since Levi's dad got here, I see the corners of his lips curve into the semblance of a smile that creeps me out. I didn't think it was possible, but the guy's mean face is actually better than his happy face.

"We've missed you around here," Dr. Close says as they pat each other on the back.

"Of course you have." Dr. William scans his surroundings. "The whole place is in shambles."

Okay, that's it. The man needs to get his eyes checked 'cause I've never seen the hospital this organized since I started working here.

"Actually, Levi has been doing a fantastic job of holding this place together," Dr. Close says.

"I highly doubt that."

"You heard about the mayor's daughter's surgery, right? Went off without a hitch, all thanks to Levi here."

"A decent neurosurgeon is supposed to know how to perform a craniotomy without any hitch, so that's nothing extraordinary," Dr. William grunts in response.

Dr. Close gives Levi a look that says "I tried, buddy," to which Levi gives him a slight nod of appreciation.

"Dad, maybe we should go to my office so you can relax a little."

"Nonsense. Take me to the OR, I want to see the circus you've got going on in there."

I can almost see Levi wince in pain as we walk through the doors of the OR to the viewing center where Dr. Thorne is implanting Brian Davis' pacemaker.

"You allow your residents to perform solo surgeries now?"

"Dr. Thorne isn't a resident, you know she's a licensed pediatric surgeon. Besides, she's successfully done pacemaker implantations more than enough times for me to trust her to do it without any supervision."

"If she's as skilled as you claim, why is she making an axillary incision instead of subclavicular?"

"I'm sure she has her reasons."

"Or maybe, hear me out, she doesn't know what the hell she's doing. What third-tier medical school did she graduate from?" he asks with a chuckle.

Levi narrows his eyes. "I'll have you know she attended and graduated with honors from Harvard."

"Hmmm. I guess Harvard hands out MDs to every Tom, Dick, and Harry that walks through their doors these days. Can I see the patient's chart?"

"No, Dad, you cannot. You still remember that little thing called doctor-patient confidentiality, don't you?"

Dr. William doesn't look pleased with Levi's response, but he knows he has him by the jugular so he doesn't say anything else. Except now, the tension between them is so thick I'm afraid it might blow up in my face any second.

"The patient has previous scarring around his clavicle."

Levi and his dad both look at me at the same time and I feel like I'm standing between the proverbial devil and the deep blue sea.

"I was working with her on his case before I, you know—"

"Almost killed him?" Dr. William offers, smacking his lips together.

"The patient has scarring from a former procedure, that's why Dr. Thorne chose the axillary incision," I finish, tucking my hair behind my ear.

"She could've chosen the inframammary incision, only lazy surgeons opt for axillary."

What a douche!

"Let's get out of here, I've seen enough desecration of my OR for today."

The three of us walk out of the OR in utter silence and as we walk down the corridor toward the elevator, Jolie calls to us from the door of a patient's room.

"Dr. Greenwood, do you have a second? I want to consult with you about a patient."

"Oh, thank God," the older Greenwood says and starts moving toward the nurse.

"I'm sorry, I meant Dr. Levi, not you, Dr. William," she clarifies, and I see his ego sink to the bottom of the ocean.

Despite the mix-up, he goes to stand within earshot of the consultation.

"You should try another anti-epileptic drug or even a vagus nerve stimulation on that patient before concluding on a surgical procedure," William Greenwood says as soon as his son exits the patient's room.

"In this case, I think surgery is the best course of action."

"From what I overheard, she doesn't have any insurance and her parents don't look like they can afford the type of procedure you're proposing," he presses on.

"And that's why the hospital has pro bono funding," I say absentmindedly, but quickly recoil when Dr. William shoots an almost murderous glare my way.

"What the hell is she talking about? What pro bono funding?"

Uh-oh, my big mouth has gotten Levi in serious trouble.

Levi shoves his hands into his pockets. "It's our way of giving back to the community."

"This is a hospital, for crying out loud, not a community center. How will my hospital make enough profit to stay open when you're handing out free surgeries like they're candy at a fucking children's party?"

Levi looks his dad square in the face, eyes hard as steel. "But it's not your hospital anymore, is it? You handed me the reins of Greenwood Hospital a year ago, so you can't tell me what I can or can't do. I run this hospital how I see fit, and there's nothing you can do about it."

For a second, I wait for the walls around us to cave in, a hurricane to sweep through, or some other sort of world-ending catastrophic event, but nothing happens. Just silence, the kind where you can hear a pin drop.

Then Dr. William turns around and walks right through the doors of the hospital.

Watching Levi stand up to his dad affects me strangely. I want to pull him close to me, interlace my fingers behind his neck, close my eyes and press my lips against his.

I catch myself just in time to hear him say, "Just so you know, I didn't tell my dad about Brian."

Who cares? You've just stood up to your dad who is one of the biggest bullies I've encountered in recent times. You're my freaking hero.

I swallow in an attempt to sound as casual as possible. "It doesn't matter. He's gone. Everything is right with the world again."

Chapter Eight

♥

Levi

To say the past few days have been grueling is a bit of an understatement. I'm so tired that I feel like once I shut my eyes, it will take me a week to open them again.

I take a sip of my sixth cup of black coffee with two sugars for the day, and lean back into my chair. I've survived today on just coffee and protein bars.

A good home-cooked meal and a hot shower in my huge bathroom sound good right about now, but remembering that those two things come with my dad in the vicinity makes me decide otherwise.

I have a perfectly good couch in my office where I can lie down and get some rest. Plus, the shower in my office—although a bit cramped—is working perfectly fine and I have a fresh pair of clothes to change into for tomorrow.

With more than half of the patients discharged and half of my staff gone for the night, I hope to have a quiet and pleasant night if my prayer for no emergency cases is answered.

Making sure my door is locked, I hop into the shower to quickly rinse off the stench of the day's activity. The warm water running down the full length of my body feels good, like a woman's touch after a long day at work.

Am I sure I know what a woman's touch feels like anymore? I chuckle to myself. It's a legit question considering the last time I had a woman's body on mine was four years ago after I ended things with Stella.

Not like I haven't had the urge to be with a woman since then, I just haven't had the time. Three years of caring for my sick mom and two working with my dad will do that to you.

A splash of cold water jerks me back to the present and has me shrinking back from the shower. I guess I spent too long fantasizing about the next time I'd feel a woman's soft bosom—preferably Lilian's—against my hard chest to notice that the hot water had run out.

Dammit, Levi. Not again.

I can't help my train of thought though, not when she and I practically spent the whole day dangerously close to each other.

Not even Dad's hostile glares or mean words stopped me from noticing how strikingly beautiful and fresh-faced she looked all day, how her brown eyes lit up when she saw my dad.

That admiration was quickly thwarted but still, I couldn't help but think how her eyes are the most beautiful I've ever looked into.

Her lips, coated with light pink lipstick, were the recipient of my lustful gaze whenever they moved. Despite her words getting me in trouble most of the time, I still wanted to take her lips in my mouth and kiss her until she swooned.

And what fresh hell was that perfume she was wearing? It was so intoxicating I had to physically restrain myself from pressing my nose against her neck and taking several deep breaths.

Looking down in frustration at the growing spectator underneath my torso, I dry my body and throw on my clothes.

I move toward the door to unlock it when I hear an announcement over the intercom in my office.

"Paging Dr. Greenwood. Dr. Greenwood, please report to the ER for a severe poisoning case. The patient, Chloe Morgan, requires immediate attention."

I push down the button on the intercom. "This is Dr. Greenwood, I'm on my way to the ER right now."

When I get to the ER, the strong smell of chlorine bleach hits my nostrils, which means that the young girl lying unconscious on one of the ER beds has ingested a copious amount of it.

Lilian is standing by her bedside with one of the night shift nurses, and updates me as soon as she sees me. "She ingested a significant amount of bleach and although we've performed a gastric lavage, she isn't responding."

"Exactly how much bleach did she ingest?" I ask, leaning in to assess the young girl.

"Almost a liter."

"Jesus!"

Chloe's hands are cold to my touch, her pupils are fixed and dilated, and her oxygen level is alarmingly low.

"Quick, let's intubate and get her oxygen levels up."

As soon as the intubation kit is handed to me, I secure the tube and attach it to a ventilator while the nurse secures the IV line.

In no time, we administer some normal saline drip to prevent dehydration and help maintain her blood pressure, and some H2 blockers to help protect her stomach lining from corrosion.

We also add some pain meds and anti-nausea medication because the last thing she needs is to regain consciousness and begin throwing up.

I study the vital signs monitor and I'm glad to see that even though she hasn't regained consciousness, her oxygen levels have significantly increased and her blood pressure has risen to an encouraging number. I instruct that once admitting orders are completed, the patient can be shifted to the ICU.

Taking off my gloves, I step out from behind the curtain to find her parents roaming the waiting room.

"Doctor, how is our daughter doing? Is she going to be okay?" He turns to his wife. "You better pray she's okay. I don't know how you could've let this happen."

"I already told you that Eliza left the bleach out where Chloe could reach it. She always keeps it out of Chloe's reach after cleaning."

"Eliza isn't her mother, you are!"

"Mr. and Mrs. Morgan, this isn't the time to play the blame game. You both need to keep it together for your daughter's sake," I say, having been a witness to such fights countless times.

"Please, how is she?" Mrs. Morgan asks again, biting back her tears.

"We've done all we can for her for now, we just need to keep monitoring her to make sure there are no further complications," I reassure her.

"I'd like my daughter to be wheeled up to the VIP floor if possible."

"Right away," I say, giving instructions to Lilian and Phil to wheel Chloe Morgan—who I now realize is the daughter of Neil Morgan, one of the wealthiest men in Elvesridge—up to the third floor.

Fifteen minutes later, as I sit hunched over my desk, slightly annoyed that the emergency with Chloe has sent sleep far from me, I hear a soft knock on my door and Lilian walks in.

"I don't bite, you know," I say when I notice she's standing awkwardly near the door. "You can sit down if you like."

She takes a seat on the couch farthest from me. "I just came by to
see if you needed anything," she says, and her stomach growls loudly.

I chuckle. "No, I don't, but clearly you need to eat something.
If you're like me, you've probably had next to nothing to eat since
morning."

She smiles. "You're right, I haven't had a decent meal all day."

"We should get some food from the cafeteria then."

She shakes her head no. "I don't feel like cafeteria food. I'm in the
mood for some chicken wings."

"Deal," I say, picking up the phone to order the chicken wings.

"While I have you here, can you go through Chloe's CT scan results
and tell me what you see?" I walk over to her and hand her my iPad,
plopping down beside her on the long couch.

She's still in her blue scrubs and somehow, after all we've been
through today, she still smells like a mix of tropical fruits and a hint
of sandalwood.

Like I said—intoxicating.

I watch her as she studies the patient's chart, her lips pressed together, eyelashes fluttering with interest.

"From what I can see, she has a thickened esophageal wall, there are
some ulcerations in her stomach lining, a discoloration of the mucosal
lining, but at least there's no fluid or air in the abdominal cavity which
means none of her organs are perforated—which is good, because it
means she doesn't need surgery."

"You got all that in less than a minute? Aiden was right, you are
brilliant."

Her cheeks redden, blending in with the rosy hue of her lips. Those lips that I've been aching to have on mine again ever since I had a taste of them.

"I'm sorry for being a total jackass today. My dad brings out the worst in me."

"You don't have to apologize, I have one of those."

"Who?"

"My mom."

"I guess parents who want to control us is another thing we have in common."

"Oh yeah? What's the first one?"

"Flaming Lips," I say, my eyes promptly lowering to hers.

She bites softly on her lower lip, which I take as an invitation to ravish her, but when I lean in, she turns away.

"Who was the blonde girl I saw you kissing the other day?"

Her question throws me completely off guard and I'm left staring at her like an idiot.

"The blonde tall one, she kissed you near the elevator."

"Oh...that was my inappropriate cousin Jenna," I reply, and I can see the relief wash over her face.

I move closer to her. "Were you jealous?"

She swallows. "Of course not."

"Oh really?" I ask, my face now mere inches from hers.

She shakes her head no, but her big brown eyes are telling an entirely different story. Being this close to her and not kissing her is torture, so I decide to end it.

I press my lips against hers and she inhales sharply, parting her lips to let me in. Slowly, wanting to savor every second, I suck on her lower lip before moving on to the upper one and then sliding my tongue into her mouth, eager to taste her.

She matches my fire, her tongue darting around in my mouth like she's trying to reach for my soul, our lips so perfectly fitted it feels like they were created for each other.

With the way her hands are tugging at my hair, I can tell she's been wanting this as much as I have, and with that realization, I pull her even closer.

Her rounded breasts crush against my hard chest, sending a cold shiver down my spine. Unable to restrain myself any longer, I let my hands trail from her neck down to her petite waist and into her scrubs, making my way up to those breasts that have driven me crazy for so long.

I graze my fingers over her taut nipples and her breath catches in her throat, a soft moan escaping from her lips. Without a second's thought, I unhook her bra and push it aside, groaning as her bare breasts come in contact with my palms. Using my thumb and index finger, I tease her nipples. She moans, tightening her grip on my hair.

Desperate to replace my fingers with my lips, I gently lift her blouse. Just as I'm about to uncover the subjects of my fantasies for the past few weeks, a knock on the door reels us back to the present.

I get up, ready to choke out whoever it is, and it's the delivery guy with the food I ordered.

Taking the food from him, I pay and shut the door, hoping to continue from where we stopped. But Lilian is already on her feet.

"I think we better go check on Chloe and see how she's doing," she says, hurrying past me.

"Fuck!" I swear, adjusting my dick which is straining against my jeans.

I can't believe I just got cock-blocked by a damn delivery boy.

Chapter Nine

♥

Lilian

This has got to be the best breakfast I've had since I came back to Elvesridge, I think to myself as I take a bite of my omelet with beef and chives accompanied by a cup of decent coffee.

"Ma'am, do you need anything else?" a chirpy waitress asks me.

"Not for now, thank you."

"Enjoy the rest of your meal," she says, her perfectly white set of teeth on display.

All the waitresses since I walked in here are so cheery, walking around with a broad smile plastered on their faces—fitting since the name of the establishment is The Sunshine Café.

Fox News, which I assume plays all day, is showing on the only TV in the café and old timers are shuffling around in their faded blue jeans, many of them coming over to me to say hi and welcome me back to town.

Suffice it to say that the only place in Elvesridge where I've experienced any rudeness is at the hospital, and that's where I get to spend most of my days and some nights. *Lucky me!*

The doorbell chimes and I look up in time to see Levi walk in, wearing a long-sleeved baby-blue shirt tucked into deep blue jeans. The shirt is tapered, showing off his slim waist and outlines of his rock-hard abs.

When he sees me and starts toward me, my insides turn to mush and I instinctively raise my hand to run it through my hair before remembering it's pulled into a tight pony so I pretend to scratch my forehead instead.

"Seems like we had the same idea, grab a quick breakfast before going in to work," he says, flashing me a casual smile.

"Don't you have like a slew of chefs back home to make you any breakfast you want?" I ask, taking a sip of my coffee.

"I could ask you the same thing."

"The only difference is you're the boss, no one will rip your head off if you show up a few minutes late. I, on the other hand, do not have that luxury."

He raises his eyebrow. "I'm your boss, are you saying I'm mean?"

Just then, one of the waitresses walks up to our table. "Hi, Dr. Greenwood, what can I get you?"

"Sofie, I've told you countless times to call me Levi."

Sofie blushes. "Sorry, force of habit."

He looks at my plate. "I'll have whatever she's having."

"You got it, Levi."

After she leaves, I check under the table to make sure she didn't drop her panties at his feet by any chance because she was practically eye-fucking him.

C'mon, Lilian, jealousy isn't a good color on you.

"So...about the other night," he says, and my heart does a backflip into my mouth. "You ran out on me so fast. I'm sorry if I crossed any lines."

"It wasn't that at all," I reply, a little faster than I intended. "It just wasn't the time or the place."

I watch his blue eyes go a shade darker so I hurry to change the subject.

"So, I know your dad was, excuse my French, horrible the other day, but his criticisms got me thinking and I have a few ideas on how to improve upon the hospital's adminis—"

"Let me stop you right there. I don't need you or my dad telling me how to run my hospital."

"That wasn't my intention."

"Just stick to patient care and leave administrative work for the experts."

I blink rapidly, taken aback by the sudden change in his tone. Nice Levi is gone, replaced by a meaner, closed-off Levi.

I down the rest of my coffee. "See you at the hospital."

"How will you get there? I didn't see your car up front."

"I'll walk."

"What about your boss ripping your head off for coming in late?"

"Worth it," I say, slamming a twenty-dollar bill on the table.

When I get to the hospital—took a taxi, by the way—Levi isn't there yet, so I decide to check in on Chloe Morgan. She's doing much better now, the swelling in her esophageal wall has gone down significantly and her wounds are healing nicely.

Leaving her room, I decide to head toward the cafeteria to grab another cup of coffee. I'll need enough caffeine in my system to deal with Levi when he gets in.

I don't understand the man—one second he's all hot and heavy and the next he's cold as ice.

"Lilian Weatherby?" I hear someone say, and I turn to see my high school bestie Laney Fields.

"I didn't know you were back in town or working here," she says after we hug.

"Yeah, I came back a month ago."

"One month? And you never asked about me."

"I'm sorry, Lane. I've been awfully busy."

"Being a badass neurosurgeon I see."

I don't correct her on the neurosurgeon thing.

"You're coming for our high school reunion Sunday night, right?" I start to say no, but she cuts in. "You have to, everyone has missed you and it will be wonderful to catch up." She takes out her phone from her purse. "I'm putting you down as my plus one so now you can't say no."

"Okay, fine."

"Yay! See you Sunday night then."

The rest of my week is spent avoiding any personal interaction with Levi, which is hard considering we're always together. By the time Sunday rolls around, I'm ready to take a break from all the tension between us.

Walking into the gym of Elvesridge High School, I see some familiar faces. I look around for Laney and soon enough, I see her walking toward me.

"Lily, you look amazing."

"Thanks Lane, you too."

"Come on, everyone's been asking about you," she says, dragging me toward a group of women.

"Hey everyone, Lily made it."

A plethora of greetings fills the air as we exchange pleasantries.

"Hi, Lil," Macy, one of my greatest bullies back in school, greets me. "Heard you were back in town, didn't believe it."

"I decided the people of Elvesridge needed more doctors than those in New York."

"Really? So you mean to tell us you left New York of your own volition?"

"Of course, why else would I leave?"

"My husband's best friend's sister, Kelsey Brent, told me an entirely different story."

I'm sure the look in my eyes is fire and brimstone because Macy decides to move on to another aspect of my life. "Most of us here are married with kids. How about you, Lil, any husband? Kids? Or are you dating someone right now?"

I'm about to tell Macy where she can shove her question when I feel a strong hand snake around my waist, followed by a kiss on the lips.

"I'm so sorry, sweetheart, finding a parking spot took longer than I expected."

"Dr. Greenwood?" Macy says, her eyes wide with surprise.

I look around and the looks of shock and envy on their faces are priceless.

"Ladies, if you would excuse me I'd love to dance with my date."

"Thanks for inviting me, Lane."

"You're very welcome. Call me."

I can still feel their eyes on me as Levi and I walk away.

"Not that I don't appreciate you being my knight in shining armor, but what are you doing here?"

"My class is also having a reunion at the alumni center and I came to check if one of my protégés made it when I saw you in the middle of those ladies and figured you needed a lifeline."

"You just figured?" I ask, arching an eyebrow in skepticism.

"I've been to a lot of these reunions. They say it's an opportunity to catch up with your old friends and classmates, but really it's a way to measure who's doing better than who."

Levi suddenly stops, taking my hands in his. "Since I already told your friends we were going to dance, let's give them a show, shall we?"

Before I can object, he slides his hand behind my back and pulls me closer to himself, his smoky scent making my head swoon.

As we twirl around on the dance floor, I can feel every movement he's making, every breath he's taking, and the way his blue eyes are glistening in the colorful hues of the strobe lights.

I know that if I spend one more second this close to him, I will say or do something that I'll regret.

"I'm sorry, I have to go," I blurt out, removing my hands from his and fleeing the room.

Chapter Ten

♥

Levi

I run after Lilian. For someone with legs half as long as mine, she's very fast. By the time I get to the space in the school field reserved for parking, I see her driving off in her brown Ford.

"Fuck," I whisper under my breath as I see one of my classmates, drunk as a skunk, staggering toward me.

It's Owen, notorious for his lewd jokes and talkativeness.

"Levi!" he says, slapping my shoulder. Who was that hot piece of ass you were running after? Is she your girlfriend?"

"No, Owen, she's not."

"So I can take her off your hands then?"

"Yeah, that's if Aiden, her older brother, doesn't chop them off first."

"You sound like you want to chop them off yourself." He burps, the stench of alcohol on his breath hitting my nostrils.

"Maybe you should go home to your wife Susan, remember her?"

"What she doesn't know won't hurt her."

Before I can respond, not that I'm eager to, my phone beeps and I pull it out of my suit pocket to see a text from Anna, my younger sister.

It reads: *I'm home bro. Where the hell are you? Ps: You need to come home now, Dad is being a pain in my ass, as usual.*

I smile and text her back: *On my way.*

"Leaving without saying goodbye? Rude." Owen snickers at me as I head toward my car.

As I drive home, I think back to the comment I made to Owen about Aiden chopping off his hands if he touches his sister. I can't help but wonder how he'd react if he found out that I've kissed the sister he begged me to employ, not once but twice. To be honest, I would have done more if that delivery boy hadn't interrupted us.

Maybe this is a sign for me to take my mind and hands off Lilian.

The only problem is I can't seem to stop thinking about her, and yet I can't seem to completely let her in either.

Relationships are a distraction. If you ever hope to hold a torch to my career, you have to focus on your career and nothing else, Dad would always say to me.

Maybe that's why his marriage to my mom was a long but unhappy one. Dad always put his career first. I vividly remember one time that Dad forgot their anniversary—he always did, but made up for it a day or two later. This time around, a week passed and he didn't even realize what had happened.

I think that was the beginning of the end. Had Mom not passed, I'm sure they'd be divorced by now.

Mom was certainly no saint, but at least she put in some effort.

As I pull into my driveway, I banish all thoughts of Lilian from my head and open the door to my living room.

"Uncle Levi! Uncle Levi!" two kids shriek as they run toward me.

"Who are you and what have you done with my niece and nephew?" I say, struggling to pick them up.

"It's us, Uncle Levi," my nephew Sam says with a giggle.

"No, it's not. You guys are three times taller than the last time I saw you."

"That's because you saw us last Christmas, it's been ten months since then," my niece Emilia—named after my mom—chimes in.

"You don't say. Where's your mom?"

"Right here," Anna says, walking out of the kitchen.

"Mommy, can you believe Uncle Levi didn't recognize us?" Sam yells in excitement.

"How could he when he only sees you two once or twice a year?"

"Ouch," I say, setting the twins down.

"Hey you," Anna says, kissing my cheeks. "You look unusually dashing."

"Unusually? I would have you know I'm the most eligible bachelor in all of Elvesridge."

"I hope you're this dressed up because you're coming from a date?"

"Sorry to dash your hopes. High school reunion, unfortunately."

"Mommy, what's a bachelor?" Emilia asks, a puzzled look on her face.

"A bachelor is a grown man who's old enough to get married and start a family but has refused to do so."

"Just like Uncle Levi," my nephew says in a sing-song voice.

"I thought us gentlemen had each other's backs," I say, and Sam laughs.

"We want a cousin, Uncle Levi," they say before running off in pursuit of each other.

I look around. "Speaking of gentlemen, where's my brother-in-law?"

Anna sighs. "He couldn't make it for Thanksgiving this year. You know how his job can be, last-minute emergency but he sends his regards."

I study her face intently. "Are you and Shawn okay?"

"Of course we are. It's tough sometimes because our schedules can be crazy, but we will get through, we always do. What about you? Any Mrs. Greenwood on the horizon?"

I clear my throat. "How's the practice doing?"

"Uh-oh, someone is trying to avoid the subject of his relationship status I see."

"Yep, I wouldn't want to poke that wildfire."

Putting my arm around her, we go to check on the kids and see what they're up to.

"So how have things been with Dad? He seems a bit cranky today."

"He's always cranky these days, nothing I say or do is good enough for him. I've had to let go of four caregivers this month alone because they all run away whenever he opens his mouth."

I see a cloud pass over my sister's face. "Mom's passing was really tough on him, and the rheumatoid arthritis diagnosis was the nail in the coffin. Maybe I should move back home and take care of him myself. Seeing his grandkids more regularly could do him some good."

"Nonsense. Your life, and the kids' lives, are in Chicago. You can't pack them up and move here because of Dad. I can handle him, I just wish he would be kinder with his words sometimes, you know?"

Anna flashes me a smile of recognition. "I do know. So tell me everything that's been happening since you took over the hospital, do not spare any details."

The next morning, I wake up to the smell of freshly baked gingerbread cake. I walk into the kitchen to see an average-sized gingerbread cake and some gingerbread cookies lying on a tray.

"Did you make these?" I ask, taking a bite of the cookies.

Anna smiles and nods. "I know how much you love these, so I decided to make them."

"Oh wow. That feels like heaven melting in my mouth. It's stupid that people wait till Christmas to eat something this delicious. If I could have something this delicious every day, I would."

Anna laughs and brings out the last batch of cookies from the oven.

"So do you have time to visit the hospital with me today? There's something important I want to show you."

"Sure. Let me just get the twins ready so we can leave."

"What's all this?" Anna asks when I lead her to a section of the hospital laboratory an hour later.

"I've been doing some research on rheumatoid arthritis."

"What kind of research?"

"I'm trying to discover ways to develop tailored treatments based on a person's genetic and molecular profile so that the side effects from the medications would be minimal. The medications help but the side effects can sometimes be as brutal as the disease itself."

Anna nods along with me. "Dad told me he developed ulcers from the medication."

"Yeah, and his blood pressure has been through the roof since he started taking them plus his doctor told us there's a risk for kidney problems with long-term use. But that's not all. I'm also trying to develop methods to identify people at high risk for developing the disease and how the onset can be prevented or delayed."

"Wow. Levi, this is huge," she says, looking through my findings so far. "Does Dad know about this?"

"God, no. He would shit all over it before it even takes off."

She flips through some more pages. "And you're doing this alone?"

"Yeah, at least until I get funding from a research institute. Although my lab technician lends me a helping hand from time to time."

Anna cocks her eyebrow at me. "What about your assistant? You told me she's brilliant. Can't she help you with the research?"

"This is unpaid work, I don't think she'll be willing to spend more hours after her regular shift doing something that doesn't come with any benefits."

Just then, as if on cue, Lilian walks into the laboratory.

"There you are, Dr. Greenwood, I've been looking all over for you. Chloe Morgan is ready to go home and her parents want to thank you before they leave."

"Please tell them I'm very busy."

"If you say so."

"Hi, Lilian. I'm Anna Greenwood, Levi's younger sister."

"Pleasure to meet you, Anna. I would never have guessed you were siblings except maybe for the similar hair color."

"Yeah, we get that a lot. Levi looks like our dad and I was fortunate to get our mom's looks."

"Your mom must've been a very beautiful woman."

"Brilliant and charming, I like you. So my brother here wanted to ask you something, didn't you, Levi?" Anna turns to look at me and I give her a *don't you dare* glare.

When the two of them keep looking at me expectantly, I cave. "So, I'm currently doing a little research—

"He means to say groundbreaking research," Anna interjects.

"...on rheumatoid arthritis and I was wondering if you would like to be a part of it."

Lilian smiles. "You had me at research."

"Really? Did I mention that it involves long hours and there's no pay whatsoever?"

"Doesn't matter, I'm down for anything that advances medicine."

"Alright then, I'll fill you in on other details later," I say before she leaves the laboratory.

Anna clears her throat. "What was that?"

"What was what?"

"You could barely look her in the eyes the whole time."

I start toward the door. "You know how weird I can be with eye contact."

"Oh no, you can't run away from this conversation," she says, walking briskly beside me. "You like her."

"No, I don't. We just work together, nothing more."

"And she likes you too."

"She does?"

Anna grins. "Why do you care if she likes you, you two just work together, right?"

I press the elevator button. "Who says I care?"

"Your eyes widening with curiosity, your face getting redder than chili peppers, should I go on?"

We step into the elevator. "You're imagining things."

"You know I worry about you, big bro. It's been ages since you ended things with Stella. It's about time you moved on and started dating again."

"When I find the right person, I will."

"I think you've found her already—maybe she's a little younger than the types you usually go for—but you two can make it work if you stop letting your pride get in the way of your happiness."

"Like I said, you're imagining things."

Chapter Eleven

♥

Lilian

When Levi said his research involved long hours, he wasn't kidding. Every day after my shifts, and sometimes during weekends, we spend a few hours talking through experiments, testing and analyzing blood and other essential tissue samples.

His sister, Anna, helps out for about a week before she has to return to Chicago with the twins. Getting to know her and learning a little about Levi's childhood has been interesting. She's carefree, cheerful, and always has a joke to tell, as opposed to Levi who is more closed off, grumpy half the time, and seldom knows how to take jokes.

After the few strenuous weeks I've had, it's amazing to hear Levi say I can clock out early for the day.

A whole evening to myself? Now that's a dream come true. I finally get to do what I've been longing to do since I came back to Elves-ridge—visit the animal shelter.

I've always been an animal lover, ever since I was a kid, but we never had a pet due to my grandparents' strict no-pet policy. While it was heartbreaking for me, there was nothing I or anyone could do. It was their house, their rules.

I had to make do with playing with Cooper, our neighbor's Rottweiler. I almost adopted a dog in New York, but I was barely getting by as it was. Plus, I was always busy.

Bringing a dog into that situation would've been terrible of me, which is why I will never understand couples who have kids when they can't afford to take good care of them.

Eventually, I settled for volunteering at animal shelters in my free time, and at one point I even joined a rebel animal activist group. That lasted like, one second, when I couldn't tell if they wanted to protect animals or just hook up with one another.

I drive home, change into a fresh pair of clothes, grab some snacks from the pantry, and head out, excited for a relaxed evening with some furry friends.

As I drive into the major road that leads to Four-Legged Haven, the animal shelter, I find it impossible not to marvel at how quiet and traffic-free the road is.

By four pm, which is usually rush hour in New York, horns would be blaring, drivers cussing at each other and at pedestrians, and people would be bumping into each other as everyone hurried back home or to go pick up their kids after closing from work.

As I get to an intersection, a car stops and waits for me to drive through even though it's well within his rights to go first. He even waves at me in greeting as I drive past him.

Such thoughtful things seldom happen in Manhattan, and are even less likely to happen during rush hour. On a whim, I decide to stop at Elvesridge Super Grocery Mart, the only major supermarket in town, to pick up some treats for the animals.

As I look around the pet supplies section, someone shopping on the same aisle catches my attention.

"Joyce?" I say, and she turns.

"Lily! Oh my God." We pull each other into a hug. "It's so great to see you." Joyce is my Aunt Florence's daughter who, ironically, is thirty-five and unmarried.

"It's great to see you too. Aiden told me you moved out of the house last summer."

She rolls her eyes. "I had to, my mom was driving me nuts."

"It's hard to believe that," I say, and we both laugh.

She looks at my hands. "So, dog treats huh? Did they finally let you get a pet in that madhouse?"

"Never. That's one decision Grams and Pops have refused to renege on. I was actually on my way to visit The Four-Legged Haven and I thought to shop for some treats. What about you, is that cat food?"

Her face lights up. "Yes, I have a cat now," she says, raising her phone to my face to show a photo of a furry black and white cat as her wallpaper.

"That's Mittens. Isn't she adorable?"

"She is. We should all hang out sometime."

"For sure. I live near Ida Sue's bakery now.

"That's cool."

"My regards to Aiden, and have fun at the shelter."

After she leaves, I pick out some treats and decide at the last minute to check the produce aisle.

Upon getting there, I'm pleased to see that the fruits and vegetables are so much cheaper than what I used to buy them for in the city.

While I bought medium-sized avocados for three dollars in Manhattan, they're a dollar for two here. I get as many as I need, pay the cashier, and drive straight to the shelter.

The first thing I notice when I walk in is that the place isn't as busy as I remember. Many of the cages are empty save for a few dogs, cats, and hamsters.

A teenage girl approaches me, all smiles. "Hello, what can I do for you?"

"I'm looking for Pete Denver? Does he still work here?"

"Actually, he owns the place now. He's currently with a visitor so who do I tell him is asking for him?"

"Lilian Weatherby."

Her eyes widen a little when she realizes who I am, which is one thing I never had to deal with in New York.

Squatting in front of one of the cages, I give one of the dogs in there a treat and he gobbles it up and starts licking my face expectantly, no doubt waiting for more treats.

"How could I say no to such a cute face?" I ask, rubbing his head as he eats the second treat.

"If I didn't know better, I'd say you were stalking me."

A shiver trails down my spine as the voice that has tormented me since the day I got into Elvesridge booms behind me.

From where I'm squatting in front of the cage, I look up at Levi and he seems even taller than usual so I stand up. Even standing, he still has about a good eight inches on me.

"I was here first, just like the other day at The Sunshine Café, so I could easily argue you're the one who's been stalking me."

"I guess we both had the same idea about what a relaxing evening should be. Nothing like the company of a furry creature to calm the nerves."

"Nothing?" I ask, and his eyes widen at the implication of my question.

"That other activity is not happening for me, seeing as the person I want is avoiding me."

I turn back to the cages as if I didn't hear him. "Cats or dogs?"

"Definitely cats."

"What? Really?"

"Yes, men enjoy the company of cats too."

"That's not what I meant, I just figured you'd be a dog person. Why, though? Why cats?"

He leans against one of the empty cages. "One word—independence. They don't require constant attention like dogs and I don't have to wake up every morning to take them out to do their business."

I shake my head. "That's the thing, I don't see why I should get a pet for companionship and want it to be independent. Cats are kinda rude too."

"That's a common misconception. They just have mood swings like the rest of us humans."

"And the scratching, how do you deal with that?" I ask, scanning him from top to bottom. "Although, you seem not to have any."

He folds his arms across his chest, making his biceps even bulkier. "That's because I don't have a cat right now. My dad, who you know is staying with me, has an allergy—or claims to have one."

"Same here. I mean, not my dad having an allergy, but my grandparents made this ridiculous rule that no one is allowed to have pets in their home."

He shrugs. "I can sort of understand why. You all are probably already too much for them to add pets into the mix."

"Hmm, you know I've never really thought of it that way," I say, running my fingers through my hair.

"How about you, besides their independence and 'rudeness' why dogs over cats?"

"They are fiercely loyal and trained to do so much. Ever heard of guide or service cats? Plus, I love my skin being scratch-free."

"Fair point. Alright, let's strike a deal."

I peer at him through narrowed eyes. "What kinda deal?"

"We switch pets. You get to spend the day with a cat and I get to spend mine with a dog. Let's see who likes the other's pet preference more."

"Okay, and what does the winner get?"

He squints his eyes. "You're one of those, huh?"

"One of who?"

"A sucker for competition."

"I mean, if there's nothing to be won, what's the point?"

He laughs. "It's not a competition, just a *Freaky Friday* sort of deal except instead of switching bodies, we switch pets."

"You should do that more often."

"Do what?"

"Laugh. It suits you."

We lock eyes and he starts to say something but then—

"Lilian Weatherby. As I live and breathe."

I turn toward Pete's voice. "And there he is. Owner of The Four-Legged Haven. Way to move up the ladder, man."

We plant kisses on each other's cheeks.

"I heard you came back to Elvesridge and I thought you'd forgotten all about us on this side of the tracks."

"Not at all. This guy," I say, nodding toward Levi, "has been working me to the bone."

"That's right. Also heard you work at Greenwood Hospital now."

"Gossip sure travels fast in Elvesridge," Levi says, and we all share a laugh.

"I'm happy your dream of being a neurosurgeon came true."

"Yeah, something like that," I say quickly, changing the conversation. "So you own the place now, huh? That's awesome. I'll be coming in here for free cuddles more often, or as often as the job allows."

Pete's face drops. "Unfortunately, that may not be possible."

Levi and I look at him at the same time. "Why not, what's going on?"

"The place is shutting down."

My eyes widen in shock. "Please tell me you're kidding."

"I wish I was. Since I bought this place from old Gregory two years ago, I've been bleeding money. Their feeding, grooming, and vet visits have all been solely on my dime. The worst part is that not many of them are getting adopted. These days people would much rather buy exotic pets than adopt one of these old fellas."

"Oh no, that's awful," Levi says, looking around at the pets.

I squat in front of a hamster's cage. "I noticed this place was a little empty, but I thought the reason was because they were getting adopted much faster."

Pete shakes his head no.

"When do you intend to shut the place down?" Levi asks, and I can tell he's unhappy about it.

"Next month."

I look at Pete. "And what do you plan to do with the remaining animals still here when you shut it down?"

"I was planning to adopt a few and hope some others get adopted. As a last resort, I was going to send them to another shelter upstate or put them down."

"We can't let that happen," Levi says, a rugged determination on his face.

Feeding off of Levi's energy, a brilliant idea pops into my head. "Umm, I think I have an idea of how to raise the money you need and get people to adopt some of these cute fellas," I blurt out, and all four eyes turn to me.

"What's this grand idea?" Pete asks, doubt written in his eyes.

"We organize a local singing competition where we can tell people all about the shelter and what will happen to these animals if they don't intervene."

They both stay quiet as if pondering my idea.

Levi nods his head first. "If done well, I think that would work."

I start pacing. "It's going to involve a lot of planning and sacrifices..."

"Not monetary, I got that covered," Levi says, and I flash him a smile.

"But I believe it will work."

"Pete?" Levi and I look at him anxiously.

"Okay, I'm in."

Chapter Twelve

❤️

Levi

What gift can I bring to a sixtieth wedding anniversary celebration? I ask myself as I drive to the Weatherby mansion.

I feel awkward about showing up empty-handed, so I decide to stop and browse through a gift shop along the way. I end up buying an old-fashioned tea set when I remember what Aiden said about his grandparents' loving antiques.

Makes sense, they're like antiques themselves. Sixty years of marriage without killing each other is no joke and is certainly worth celebrating.

Waiting till the last minute to get a gift for them wasn't intentional, I just didn't know I would be attending the party until tonight. With few patients needing my attention at the hospital, Dr. Thorne and Dr. Close assured me they had everything under control, so I decided to honor Aiden's invitation.

Besides, seeing Lilian outside the four walls of Greenwood Hospital again isn't an idea I'm mad at. Since our little rendezvous at the animal shelter, thoughts of her have just about consumed me. I want—no, *need*—to know more about her when we don't have people's brains and lives in our hands.

As I drive up to the mansion, the garden area is alive with activity. Guests are moving around helping themselves to food while others dance to the music.

In the middle of the garden is an elaborate six-tier fondant cake—one for each decade of their marriage, I'm assuming—and a giant sculpture of Aiden's grandparents sitting on it.

Dropping from some strategic points in the garden are low-hanging light bulbs illuminating the otherwise dark night.

I go into the main house and place my gift beside a pile of other gifts on the center table before joining the other guests out in the garden.

Opulently dressed guests are seated on each side of three carefully arranged long tables and one of Aiden's cousins, Ingrid, shows me to my assigned seat. Taking my seat, which is in the middle, I feel grossly underdressed in my choice of a simple shirt and trousers.

Grandma and Grandpa Weatherby are sitting at the head of the table exchanging pleasantries with some guests when Aiden, who has always been the outspoken one in the family, clinks his glass with a spoon, drawing everyone's attention to him.

"It's time for anyone who has a toast or speech about the special love between Gramps and Nana to take the floor. I know my speech is gonna be the best so I'm saving it for last."

Just as the first speech is about to start, I see Lilian walk out of the house in a strapless white gown and I momentarily lose my breath. I've only seen her in scrubs, and in tees and jeans, but seeing her walking toward the garden I can't help but be lost in her aura.

As my eyes follow her across the garden, I don't notice someone else take a seat beside me till she speaks.

"Enjoying the speech, are we?"

Oh, hell no! This has got to be a joke or a fucking nightmare.

For the first time since I sat at the table, I look at the place card a few inches away from mine, and it's real. Scribbled across the black and white place card is the name *Stella Moore*.

"Is your plan to pretend I'm not sitting next to you for the rest of the night?" she asks, and I'm forced to turn toward her.

"What are you doing here?"

"Same thing you are. I'm here to celebrate Martha and Stuart's love."

I scoff and roll my eyes. "That's fucking ironic," I say, angry that Stella made me miss Lilian's entrance.

"The fact that we didn't work out doesn't mean I stopped believing in love."

"Didn't work out? That's a very nice way to put it."

"I don't understand why you've got ants in your pants. Aiden said you wanted me here."

"And you believed him? After everything you put me through, you genuinely thought I would want anything more to do with you?" I ask, getting up from my seat. "If you'll excuse me, I need a drink."

Fucking Aiden. So this is why he was so insistent I come? And here I was hoping he had somehow developed superpowers to know I liked his sister—which is stupid because if he knew, he'd be ripping my head off not inviting me to his house.

I decide to have my drink under one of the maple trees. Anywhere is better than being near Stella for another second.

From where I'm standing I can see Aiden's grandparents and some other guests twirling around the dance floor with their partners and dates.

"I don't think your date will appreciate you standing here instead of with her on the dance floor."

Despite my foul mood, hearing Lilian's voice instantly makes me feel like I just successfully performed a brain tumor resection.

I look over at Stella and notice she's talking with some other guy at our table.

"I don't think she knows I'm gone."

"So she is your date."

I turn to face Lilian and she's even more beautiful up close. Her blonde hair is hanging loose over her shoulders, a little sunflower tucked in beside her ear, and her brown eyes are sparkling with the reflection from the lights. The urge to kiss her suddenly rises in me and I sip my drink to mask it.

"Why do you care if I came with her?"

"Who says I cared? I was just being curious."

I stifle a smile "She's not my date. This little arrangement you see here is courtesy of your brother."

She's wearing a puzzled expression so I explain further. "Stella is my ex-fiancée."

"You have an ex-fiancée?" she asks, eyebrows shooting up in surprise.

"Can you not look so surprised that someone actually dated me?"

She winces. "Sorry. So what happened? Did you get cold feet?"

"Nope." I take another sip from my glass. "She left me a day before our wedding."

"Oh God, that's awful. So why would Aiden invite her here if he knows how badly things ended with you two?"

"We were talking about regrets the other day and I mentioned my relationship with Stella. I guess he thought I meant regret over how we ended things."

"Oh. Please tell me she left a note explaining why she left?"

"Nope. Just an 'I'm sorry, I just couldn't marry you' text four days after the fact."

Lilian is looking at me with the pity I see on people's faces whenever I tell them about Stella leaving me.

"Don't feel sorry for me, it was for the best. When I got over the pain and looked at things more clearly, I realized that Stella was never the one. I didn't feel butterflies whenever she was around me, her smile never lit up a room for me, and I didn't look forward to seeing her every day. She never gave me those feelings you feel when you love someone."

"And yet you would have married her if she hadn't left you."

I shrug. "Probably. I was young. I thought I was in love, and my plan was always to graduate medical school, do my residency, fellowship, and get married."

She looks away, a shadow crossing her face. "I guess things don't always work out how we plan them in our heads, huh."

I clear my throat. "So now that we've talked about the most embarrassing moment of my life, can I ask you a question?"

She nods affirmatively. "Sure."

"At the animal shelter the other day, Pete said something about your dream of being a neurosurgeon coming true. What did he mean by that?" She looks petrified, like I'm asking her to expose her deepest, darkest secret, so I quickly add, "You don't have to tell me, I'm just curious."

"I was a second-year resident neurosurgeon at Mount Sinai Hospital. One of the best and brightest in my set according to the chair of surgery, Dr. Roberts. I guess I got it into my head that I could perform my very first surgery—a spinal fusion—solo. And unfortunately, I had a supervisor crazy enough not to stop me."

She pauses and I can tell that this next part is painful for her to share. "Needless to say, I was in way over my head, and during the surgery, my scalpel veered off course and I nicked a nerve on the patient's lumbar spine. Patrick Brenner ended up paralyzed, in a wheelchair, unable to play with his then two- and four-year-old daughters. Dr. Roberts, my supervisor, was fired and the hospital paid through their nose to settle Patrick's lawsuit."

"The way I see it, none of it was your fault. Residents can be ignorantly arrogant sometimes and that's the reason they're assigned a supervisor, to stop them from making decisions like this."

She disagrees with a shake of her head. "I was the one holding that scalpel when the patient got paralyzed. I don't care how anyone spins it, it was my fault. The hospital suspended me for weeks and when I came back, my confidence level in the OR dropped and I started to second-guess myself. When I became a liability in the OR instead of an asset, I knew it was time to quit. I've always loved medicine, and caring for people comes naturally to me. So deciding to become the physician's assistant you see standing before you today was a no-brainer."

She lets out some air through her mouth. "Apart from Aiden, you're the only person I've trusted enough to open up about this."

She trusts me. That's a great start.

"Your parents don't know?"

"If I told my dad, he would overreact and do too much to try and make me feel better, and telling my mom would be giving her another reason to be disappointed in me."

"So you're no longer interested in neurosurgery?"

She takes a pause and that's all I need to know her answer.

"I'm not sure if I can ever get over what I did. How does someone just move on from something like that?"

I take a deep breath. "My first patient died on my operating table. It was supposed to be a very simple procedure, short, in and out, but I royally messed it up and the patient died."

"You're kidding."

"I'm not. And do you know how many more patients I've lost since then? Fifteen. Some died during surgery, some died afterward."

"Are you trying to make me feel better or plunge me deeper into my misery?"

"Neither. I'm just trying to let you know that in this profession, we save some, and we lose some. What we don't do is quit because we lost—even if it was an avoidable mistake. Now, guess how many lives I've saved since then."

"Forty, fifty?"

"Countless. If I had quit because of that first mistake, I wouldn't have had the opportunity to save those lives. Lilian, you're brilliant and I know you'll do great as a neurosurgeon. It's not too late, you know. Think about it."

I watch her pluck a maple leaf from the tree without saying anything.

"So your grandparents have been together for sixty years and they still look at each other like that." She follows my eyes to Martha and Stuart on the dance floor and I continue, "Do you think love like theirs still exists?"

She looks up at me and I can see the hopeful gleam in her eyes. "I hope I never have to live in a world where love like theirs doesn't exist anymore."

We fall silent for a while, just watching them look at each other like the only two people in the whole world.

Chapter Thirteen

♥

Lilian

"You're so lucky, Lil. I can't believe your day off fell on the same day as the meteor shower," Laura says to me as we walk toward our cars in the parking lot.

"I know, it's amazing."

"So who are you going to watch with? It's never fun watching alone."

"My brother and I have been preparing for tomorrow night for weeks. We used to stay up late with our dad to watch the meteor showers when we were younger so it kind of became our thing."

Laura rolls her eyes. "That's so boring. You should go with someone you can kiss. Trust me when I say you've not truly lived till you've made out with a hot guy underneath the stars."

I laugh. "Unfortunately, not everyone has a sweet, hot boyfriend like you."

She leans against my car. "You know, said hot boyfriend has a few handsome friends. I could give one of them your number if you like."

I open the car door and throw my backpack in the passenger seat. "Maybe some other time."

"Alright then, have fun."

"I would say you too but we both know that a night shift on the day of a meteor shower is anything but fun."

She pokes her tongue out at me and continues toward her car.

The next morning, after I've had breakfast, I decide to drop in on Aiden and see how he's preparing for tonight. When I knock on his door, he comes out shirtless and a little sweaty.

"What's going on? Why are you sweating like that?"

"I have a lady friend in there."

"Ewww. Why did you come out then?"

He rolls his eyes. "With the way you were knocking, I felt this must be important. So what's up?"

"Just wanted to know if you've bought the beers we're taking to our thing tonight."

"About that...I'm so sorry, Lil, but I won't be able to come tonight."

"What? Why not?"

"Maureen and I have more important things to do tonight."

"Who's Maureen?"

"My girlfriend."

"I thought your girlfriend's name was Jessica."

"We broke up, I'm with Maureen now."

I fold my arms across my chest. "This is so unfair. I brought Bobby home in tenth grade to study and Mom and Dad freaked out on us so badly that Bobby developed a nosebleed. But you, they allow you to have lady friends over like we're running a brothel."

"That's because they don't know about this, so keep your voice down."

I give him a doubtful look. "So what are you and Maureen doing tonight that could be more important than us going to watch meteor showers?"

"There's this particular sex thing I've been asking—"

"Eww. Eww, don't say one more word." I block my ears with my fingers and walk away as fast as I can.

Picking sex over a chance to bond with his sister? Boys will always be boys I guess.

As the sun dips below the horizon, I decide that Aiden's decision to prioritize his "sex thing" over our sibling thing won't stop me from going to the park. I drive there solo, pick out a nice secluded spot, and spread my blanket.

There are a handful of other people at the park but, as I noticed while driving here, most people prefer to watch the meteor shower from their front yards—unlike in New York where I'm sure Central Park is filled right now.

Having spent the whole day catching up with the hours of sleep my strenuous shifts have been depriving me of, I feel deliciously alive and energized, happy to be here underneath the beautiful night sky.

Speaking of things that make me feel alive, Levi pops into my head and I smile.

The tension between us has been off the charts since the night of my grandparents' anniversary party. The more time we spend together, the more fascinating he becomes—which is funny considering our first and second meetings. I never imagined I'd feel free enough to open up to him about the most devastating period of my life, but here I am, happy that I did.

Despite how close we're getting, I'm still trying to keep the fact that I haven't been able to stop thinking about him hidden. It isn't new for

Levi to give me signals that he likes me one day and become cold the next, so I'm trying hard not to get my hopes up again.

I lie back on the blanket and close my eyes, imagining what he would look like fully unclothed, my hands tracing his chiseled abs down his torso.

"Lilian," someone whispers, and my eyes fly open.

For a second, I think I'm still imagining things, but Levi is actually here, standing before me, looking devastatingly handsome.

Also, for the first time since I met him, his hair looks gel-free, parted at the center and making him look like a younger Jake Gyllenhaal.

"What are you doing here? Don't tell me stargazing is another thing we have in common."

"Nope, I couldn't care less about stars or meteors. I was on my way home when I saw your car and I couldn't stop myself from coming to say hi. Mind if I join you?"

"Not at all," I say, adjusting myself to create some space for him.

He lies right beside me, his strong masculine scent filling the air around us. Lying this close to him, the way I've imagined for weeks, feels unreal—like I should reach out and touch him just to make sure he's really lying beside me, a few inches keeping us apart.

It's a given that we've been this close to each other on many occasions, but tonight feels different somehow. Every hair on my body is on its toes and it's taking every bit of self-control I have not to roll over and beg him to kiss me.

"This isn't half bad," he says, breaking the silence that has enveloped us.

"Of course it's not. Look at the sky, full of stars, some of them a million years old, arranged in such carefully thought out patterns." I turn my face toward him. "Have you ever seen anything more beautiful?"

"Yes I have—you," he says, his blue eyes fixated on me. "I haven't been able to stop thinking about you since that night in my office."

I feel a warm glow spread across my cheeks. "Really?"

He pulls himself an inch closer. "I spend every waking moment thinking of kissing you again, wanting to taste every inch of your gorgeous body."

"Levi," I whisper, my heart racing like a sprinter in the final stretch.

He moves closer once more till our faces are almost touching. "I want you right here...right now."

He takes my hand and places it over his groin, and when I feel his rock-hard member bulging against my palm, I'm left breathless.

"Can you feel what you do to me?" he says, his voice a kind of deep I've never heard before.

Before I can say a word, his soft lips crash into mine and all my reservations about him and his feelings for me vanish into thin air.

I let myself drown in the magic of our lips meeting in perfect symphony, let myself be swept up into the wild sensations running through my body as he teases my lips with his.

I moan into his mouth when his tongue touches mine, hot and tingly, making me forget that we're in an open park as I shamelessly grind my hips against his.

His hands, hard yet comfortable, pull my body closer to his until there's no space left between us, until we're breathing in each other's air. Setting my lips free, he trails his tongue over my jaw, licking and sucking, his tongue setting my flesh on fire as it travels down to the nape of my neck.

In one well-timed attempt, he turns me on my back, lifts my shirt, and trails kisses from my belly button up to my breasts. I arch my back and his hands go around me to unhook my bra.

I watch his eyes widen in pleasure as he peels off my lace bra. My nipples, hard and long, are pointing toward the sky, begging to be ravished.

"God, I've been dreaming of doing this since the first time we kissed."

"They're all yours now."

Like a worshiper at the feet of his god, his head falls to my chest and he takes my nipple into his mouth as my head falls back into the blanket, a deep moan escaping from the back of my throat.

I can feel my nipple getting longer and harder in his warm mouth, and just when I think I'll die from the pleasure of his tongue, his hand moves to my jeans and he unbuttons my fly.

With the last resolve left in me, I whisper, "Are you sure you want to do this? Once you touch me there, there's no going back."

"Then I guess there's no going back."

Fuck, that's hot!

Unzipping my fly, he tugs down my jeans and panties, leaving me completely naked from the waist down.

His lips find my nipple again and as he sucks on it, I feel his fingers slowly part my pussy lips and find my clit.

Pushing past it, he inserts his fingers into my now dripping center, coating his fingers with my juices and bringing them back up to tease my love button.

I've heard rumors about surgeons' hands being gifted, not only in the OR but in the act of pleasuring a woman, and from the fire coursing through my veins at this very moment I can say that whoever started those rumors told no lies.

Not even a little bit.

As Levi's fingers alternate between fucking me and sliding back and forth on my now swollen clit, his tongue and teeth are giving my nipples sensations they have never felt before and the pleasure is getting to be too much for my poor body to bear.

Like tidal waves, waves of pleasure rise higher and higher inside me and I know I'm close to exploding on Levi's hands.

"Don't stop, please don't stop," I cry as he intensifies the movement of his fingers over my clit.

He dips his fingers into my pussy one last time and as he flicks them over my clit, I get to the point of no return, my body shuddering, toes curling as waves and waves of pleasure flow through me like a tsunami. Levi holds me till my body stops shaking and I catch my breath.

Impatiently, I tug at his jeans, letting him know that I want him inside me. As I watch him struggle to pull down his jeans, I place my arm over his and gently push him down till he's lying on his back.

I tug on the jeans and briefs and when his dick, firm as a boulder, springs out of his briefs, a gasp escapes my lips.

"Are you protected?"

"Yes, I'm on the pill."

"Oh thank God 'cause I need you so fucking bad."

Eager to feel his entire length inside me, I straddle him and he holds himself steady as I gently lower myself onto him, his erection filling up every inch of my dripping pussy in the most treacherous way.

Wanting more of the delicious pleasure rocking my entire body, I raise myself and lower myself back onto him.

He lets out a deep moan and closes his eyes, lost in the pleasure rising between us.

As I try to increase the pace, he holds me in place. "Lily…fuck…you're too sweet, if you move any faster you're going to make me cum, and I don't want to cum just yet."

There's something about the way he's pleading that sends a warm sensation flooding through my entire body.

"Then control the pace," I say, and he grabs my ass, gently lifting me and lowering me back down. I throw my head back, letting myself feel every stroke, every thrust, as little by little, he increases the pace.

Soon he thrusts his hips upward and takes over completely, thrusting in and out of me mercilessly.

"Fuck, Lily, I don't want this feeling to end," he cries out, and I can see from the pleasure lines etched into his face that he's about to cum.

"Fuuuck! I'm cumming, baby," he says, grabbing my ass so tight as his hips buck wildly underneath me.

He sighs in satisfaction and at that exact moment, I see a flashing light and look up to see meteors racing across the starlit sky.

"Beautiful," he says.

"I know, right?"

"I meant you."

I place a kiss on his lips and gently lift myself off him, lying beside him and placing my neck in the crook of his arm.

"Did you ever think you'd make love underneath the skies?"

I shake my head no. "Not even in a million years."

Last night, Laura told me that you've never truly lived until you kissed a guy underneath the stars. I guess tonight I lived twice.

As I lie here in Levi's arms, his heart thumping against my ears, breathing in his delicious scent and watching meteors shoot across the sky, for the first time since I returned to Elvesridge, I feel like everything is going to be okay.

Chapter Fourteen

Levi

Last night was one of the most amazing nights of my life, right up there with the day I officially got my license to become a practicing neurosurgeon.

I finally got to make love to the most beautiful woman I've ever laid eyes on, underneath a starlit sky in a public park. I should be throwing a fucking rager right now to celebrate, but my anxiety is through the roof.

Any minute now, Aiden will walk into the gym and we'll shake hands, probably hug like we always do before starting our workouts, and he'll have no clue that I've broken a pact we made years ago to never get involved with each other's sister.

It may have been a pact we made as teenagers, but knowing Aiden, I'm sure he meant every word. The excuse of "*We were young, I thought we were just goofing around*" won't fly with him.

But the worst part isn't even me breaking our pact. The worst part is that despite feeling awful, I want to do it over and over again, consequences be damned.

"Hey, man." Aiden touches my shoulder and I jump with fright.

My attention has been at the door, expecting him to walk in, not knowing that he was already here.

"Jesus, man! When did you get here?" I ask, managing to regain my composure.

"I came in a little early to talk with Kyle about fixing some spoiled equipment. So what nasty thing did you do yesterday?"

My heart skips a beat. "What? Did anyone tell you I did something?"

"Of course not. You're acting a little strange, man. Is everything okay?"

You need to get it together, Levi.

"Everything is peachy, it's just some work stuff."

"I'm sure you'll figure it out, you always do. And once again, I'm sorry for inviting Stella to my grandparents' anniversary."

I wave it off. "It's okay, man. It was just a misunderstanding."

He places a hand on my shoulder. "Misunderstanding or not, I've come up with a way to make it up to you. You and I are going on a double date tomorrow night with my girlfriend and her smoking hot friend Nancy. That is, unless you're seeing someone."

"Nope. Just text me the time and venue and I'll meet you there."

"Dude, you're gonna owe me after you meet Nancy tomorrow. She's your type—hot, tall, blonde, and insanely attractive."

"I can't wait," I say, stepping on the treadmill.

After my awkward workout session—awkward for me at least—with Aiden, I return to the hospital, and as soon as I exit from the elevator, my assistant Sam hands me my post-workout fruit smoothie.

"Your dad called and complained for over fifteen minutes about his new nurse, he said to tell you to call and fire her. Oh, and someone from the National Institutes of Health called and left a message for you."

My eyes widen in exasperation. "And you didn't think to lead with that piece of information? Jesus, Sam. What did the message say?"

"That they would get back to you tomorrow with their decision."

"That's great. Go tell Ms. Weatherby to come to my office right away."

"Um, I don't think she's coming in till five."

"Fine, tell her to come see me as soon as she gets in."

An hour later, I hear a soft knock on my door and Lilian walks in, looking as stunning as she always does despite being in her usual scrubs.

"You asked to see me," she says, sounding very formal, as if we weren't moaning into each other's mouths a few hours ago.

"Hey, no one can hear us, you can drop the formal act whenever you come in here."

She pulls her hands from her scrub pockets. "It's not an act, this is how employees talk to their boss."

I lean forward and lower my voice. "After last night, I want to believe we're a bit more than boss and employee."

"Was this why you sent for me?" she asks, and I can hear the impatience in her voice.

"No. I got a call from the NIH about the research funding proposal we sent out. They're going to get back to me by tomorrow."

"Hope you asked them what time they'd call so you won't be too busy with your date to pick up."

"Oh…you know about the date and that's why you're acting this way."

"Forgive me for thinking that yesterday meant more to you than just a booty call," she says, and I can't help but smile. "Don't laugh at me or I swear—"

I cross over to her and cut her off with a kiss.

"It doesn't matter how good a kisser you think you are, it can't fix this," she says, trying to catch her breath.

"I'm not trying to fix anything. You may not know this, but back in high school your brother and I promised each other that we would never date or even look at each other's sisters as anything more than friends. Well, I've done more than look at you, and I'm worried about how he'll react if he finds out."

She lets out an embarrassed laugh. "That's why you're going on the date, to throw him off our scent."

"Exactly."

"Levi, it's a high school pact, I'm sure he's forgotten all about it."

"This is Aiden we're talking about, he hasn't forgotten."

"Yeah, probably not."

"So, was that you being jealous?" I ask, wrapping my hands around her waist.

"You can't just make love to a girl the way you did and then go on another date the next day. It's not—"

Sam jerks the door open and we come apart faster than Lego blocks.

"Did you understand everything I explained to you, Ms. Weatherby?"

"Yes, doctor."

"Then make sure you've updated and sent me those patient files before the end of your shift tomorrow morning."

"You've got it, Dr. Greenwood," she says, hurrying out of my office.

"Yes, Sam, what is it?"

"Dr. Close wants to see you urgently, he's in the conference room."

"Alright, thanks."

That was close. I mutter to myself after Sam shuts the door behind him.

Seconds later, my phone beeps and it's a text from Aiden with the time and venue of our double date.

***

When I arrive at the Moonlite Diner, I see Aiden's sea-green Chevrolet parked outside, so I park my Mustang beside his car and enter the restaurant.

Looking around, I spot Aiden and his girlfriend sitting at a table by the window, but my date is nowhere to be found.

"Hey man, sorry I'm late. Crazy day at the hospital," I say, taking my seat.

"At least you showed up this time."

"It's been three years, man, am I ever gonna live that down?"

Aiden shakes his head. "Not a chance. Maybe in two or three years, we'll see. Babe, this is my best friend Levi, and Levi this is Maureen, my girlfriend."

We shake hands. "It's nice to finally put a beautiful face to your name."

"You were right, babe, he's a charmer. Nice to meet you too, Levi."

"So, where's my date?" I ask, hoping they'll tell me she got bored and went home.

In case you haven't guessed it already, my lateness is deliberate.

"She went to the bathroom. I think our PDA was making her a little uncomfortable, especially since her date wasn't here yet."

Maureen smiles. "Yeah, she was probably feeling like the third wheel. Oh, here she is now."

I turn around to see a tall, gorgeous blonde walking toward our table. Aiden didn't lie about her beauty, she is truly elegant and as he rightly said—my type. Yet watching her walk over to the table, I feel zero excitement.

"Hi," I greet, pulling out her seat for her. "I apologize for being late."

"No need to apologize, I understand the crazy hours doctors work. You guys are the real heroes, not the adults in tights."

"Thanks for saying that."

A waiter comes by and takes my food and drink orders since they already started without me.

"So, Aiden tells me you're a neurosurgeon, what does saving people's lives every day feel like?" Nancy asks, looking at me keenly.

"Long days, longer nights. Sometimes I spend almost a week at the hospital without going home or having time to see anyone outside the hospital, which is why dating me is a terrible idea."

"What do you mean?" Nancy asks, placing a hand on my thigh.

"Let me paint you a picture. Imagine we hit things off and start dating and you never get to see me or spend time with me except on rare occasions like holidays or my off days, and those come along once in a very long while. Now imagine that on that holiday or day off when you finally get me all to yourself for the first time in months, I get a call that there's an emergency at the hospital that requires my attention. A human being's life is at stake, so of course I'll have to go, and you wouldn't want to be selfish by asking me to stay."

Aiden shoots me a glare but I ignore him and continue.

"I tell you I'll be right back but I don't get back till five or six hours later and by then the dinner you took your time to prepare is cold and you're probably asleep on the couch where you fell asleep waiting for me."

"Wow. If that's all your life is, it's a really small one," Maureen says, her gaze fixed on me like I'm a lost puppy.

"That was why my ex left me, she said she felt like she was in a relationship with herself."

Aiden gives Maureen a signal and she and Nancy leave with the excuse of going to freshen up, leaving only the two of us at the table.

"What the hell is wrong with you, man? It sounds like you're deliberately trying to sabotage this date, and we both know Stella didn't leave you because you were always busy. Do you not like Nancy or what?"

"I do, but I think she likes me a little too much."

"I'm confused. A hot girl liking you too much isn't a good thing?"

"It is, but I don't think I'm ready for anything that serious right now."

"Well, you're in luck then, because Nancy isn't the serious relationship type either. The two of you could leave right now and go have a *fun* night."

I stand up and place some money on the table. "This should cover the cost of everything we ate and drank. Please tell Nancy I'm sorry for wasting her time."

As I drive away from the restaurant, my stomach—which has been in knots all night—finally loosens up.

Truth is, I spent the entire time thinking of Lilian and feeling like I was betraying her by being here.

Is there something seriously wrong with me or am I falling in love with Lilian Weatherby?

Chapter Fifteen

Lilian

I should be getting some rest with what little time I have before the night shift rush hour begins, but here I am lying on one of the beds in the on-call room, thinking of Levi on his stupid date.

Even though I had promised myself that I wouldn't, I made the mistake of asking Aiden about Maureen's friend and then spent my entire day stalking her on social media.

On paper, she and Levi are perfect for each other. She's physically his type. I know she's adventurous because her Insta is littered with images and videos of her going skydiving, bungee jumping, zip-lining, and other fun activities.

I'm pretty sure Levi would prefer that to someone who spends her Saturday nights either at work, sleeping, or watching reruns of *The Office.* By my count, she's been to about fifteen different countries on crazy adventures, and then there's me who can't go for a run if my life depended on it.

She's a fitness junkie just like Levi, and he'll probably take one look at her, fall for her, and forget I exist. Surely Maureen has less attractive friends that Aiden could've set Levi up with but no, he had to pick the hottest one.

When I can't take the ceiling gazing and wild thoughts anymore, I grab my phone and decide to text Levi. If he responds, I'll know there's hope for me yet, since no one looks at their phone while they're having a good time.

I type in a few messages and delete all of them because there's no way to ask Levi if he's fallen in love with her without sounding like a complete psycho.

Dropping my phone back in my locker, I opt to go check in on Mrs. Porter, one of my favorite patients in the hospital. She's been in the hospital for about a month undergoing aggressive chemotherapy and radiation for stage four breast cancer.

Despite being in constant pain and often exhausted from everything her body is going through, she always has a reassuring smile on her face and asks me how I'm doing whenever I come around to check on her.

Another thing I love about her is that she's so sure she'll walk out of here on her own two feet like she did five years ago when the cancer was first discovered. Having such strong convictions in the face of a terrible disease is truly inspiring.

Although she isn't part of my responsibility during my shifts, I always love to drop in on her for a few minutes.

When I get to her room, her bed is empty so I assume they've taken her to do some tests or scans.

Just then I see Jolie come out from another patient's room so I approach her. "Hi, Jolie."

"What do you want, Ms. Weatherby? I'm going home and can only spare a second."

It always amuses me how Jolie's name means nice in French because the woman wouldn't know nice if she ate it for breakfast, lunch, and dinner.

"I only need a second. I just came in for my shift and came to check in on Mrs. Porter but she's not in her room."

Her face goes from an annoyed glare to a concerned look, and I immediately know something is wrong.

"You haven't heard? Mrs. Porter died this morning."

"What? How?"

"She suffered multiple organ failure from sepsis and her heart took a huge hit. We tried all we could to revive her, but it was her time."

"But...but I saw her last night and she seemed to be doing much better."

Jolie touches my shoulder lightly, which is a shock to me since I didn't think the woman had any human emotions toward anyone who isn't her patient.

"Don't take it too much to heart, death is an unavoidable part of our job."

"Thanks," I manage to whisper, trying my best not to let my voice betray my emotions.

Managing to pull through my shift without randomly bursting into tears takes every atom of strength I have, and when I eventually get home, I'm so exhausted from trying to hold back my tears that I can't stop crying.

And even though I haven't gotten over Mrs. Porter's death yet, I have to go to work the next day, plaster a smile on my face, and pretend nothing happened. I manage to pull through the day without snapping at anyone or stealing a moment to cry in the on-call room, which I count as a huge victory.

After my shift, I get into my car to head home, but when I try to start it, the engine doesn't budge. I try several times and the lights don't even come on.

"Fuck! Fuck! Fuck!" I yell, resting my head on the steering wheel.

With nothing left to do, I grab my backpack and decide to walk home. Maybe the cool breeze will help me clear my head.

Just as I round the corner from the hospital onto the road, a car honks behind me and I turn around to see Levi signaling me to get in.

"Thanks, but you don't have to drop me off, you'll be late for work."

"Good thing I'm the boss then," he says, opening the passenger door for me to get in. "What happened to your car?" he asks after I've fastened my seat belt.

"It refused to start, which isn't surprising. Damn car is older than me and sometimes its age catches up to it."

"You don't seem like yourself, is something wrong?" he asks, his face marked by concern.

I thought I was doing a nice job of masking my feelings but apparently not.

"I'm fine, why would you think something's wrong?"

"Because you didn't text or call me to find out the NIH's decision about funding our research and you still haven't asked me."

Dammit, I completely forgot about the NIH.

"I'm so sorry for not asking sooner. What did they decide?"

"Not until you tell me what's bothering you."

"I don't know if you heard, Mrs. Porter died."

He gives me a confirming nod. "I heard. Dr. Close informed me that her sepsis was getting worse and defying all the treatments being given to her. After I saw her, I wasn't sure she would last till morning."

"How do you deal with losing so many patients and going about your business like nothing happened?"

He sighs deeply. "First of all, I don't go about my business like nothing happened. When I first started practicing, the death of every patient used to hit me so hard. Although the pain didn't get easier, over time I found a better way to manage it so it wouldn't affect my care for my other patients in any way." He looks over at me briefly. "You know, this is why we're always told not to get too attached to our patients, it's so their deaths don't hit us this way."

"That's one thing that never quite made sense to me. How do you care for someone, laugh with them, hope with them that they'll get better, and sometimes even cry with them, and yet you're miraculously expected not to get attached to them? It doesn't add up."

He shrugs. "It makes sense if you want to keep your sanity doing what we do every day."

"So how exactly did you learn to deal with it? The pain, I mean?"

"It's simple and yet very effective. I talk about it with a friend from my time in medical school. We kept in touch after graduating and whenever either of us loses a patient, we call the other person and talk through the pain. I feel much better afterward."

I look straight at him for the first time since I came into the car. "Do you ever regret becoming a neurosurgeon?"

Without thinking, he shakes his head no. "I don't have regrets about anything—well, maybe a little about me and Stella—but other than that, I think looking back is pointless. What about you, any regrets?"

"On rough days like yesterday and today, I regret not pursuing my interest in music instead. Sometimes I regret leaving New York, and I regret letting my failure at neurosurgery haunt me for so long."

"Why didn't you pursue music instead? You seem to know a lot about it and I've heard you sing, you have a wonderful voice."

I turn my head sharply to look at him. "You've heard me sing? When?"

"Does Lily underscore nightingale ring a bell?"

I smile. "You found me on Instagram."

"The week you started working in the hospital, or do you think I'm too old to know how to stalk someone on social media?"

"I'm impressed. I tried to find you on Instagram too, by the way. No posts whatsoever."

"Yeah. I only opened an account to check you out. I don't think I've been back there since then. So why not music?"

I scoff. "Have you met my family members? My great-grandparents were renowned scientists, my grandparents were both on Martin Luther King's legal team, my dad used to build airplanes from the ground up and my mom owns the biggest dental practice in the greater Houston metropolitan area where many of my cousins work. Even Aiden, who's considered the fuck-up of the family, after me of course, is one of the best engineers I know. Imagine what their reaction would be if I told them I wanted to become a musician."

"And I thought my family tree was impressive. Your parents don't seem like the type, they've always been very nice to me."

"That's because they don't expect anything from you."

"True. It must be a lot of pressure though, trying to live up to their expectations?"

"It can be sometimes, which is precisely why I chose not to tell them how badly I screwed things up with neurosurgery."

We've gotten to the arrow pointing to the Weatherby mansion by now and I suggest stopping here may be best.

As I'm about to get out of the car, he takes my hand in his and a wave of calm rushes over me.

"I get you, Lilian Weatherby, and working beside you almost every day I see how strong, compassionate, and amazing you are at your job. It doesn't matter what anyone else says or thinks, never forget that you're a rock star."

He leans over to kiss me and as our lips meet, I temporarily forget all my woes. His kisses, touches, and even his presence alone always have this effect on me.

"You're too amazing to live with all those regrets you mentioned, and if you truly regret going into medicine, you have a big decision ahead of you," he says after our lips part.

"At this point, I think I should start paying you for being my therapist." His lips curve into a smile. "Thanks for the lift, and everything else."

"You're welcome."

After I get out of the car, Levi waves to me and drives off, and I stand there till he's out of sight.

He's one of the nicest and sweetest guys I've ever met, though he's scary good at hiding that fact behind stern looks and words.

And he is right—I have run away from this decision long enough. It's time for me to stop hiding behind being a physician's assistant.

I have two options now—go back to neurosurgery or say consequences be damned, or pursue a career as a singer.

Chapter Sixteen

♥

Levi

W
ith the holidays fast approaching, our small town is saturated with Christmas decorations. Elvesridge is one town where Christmas celebrations are taken almost as seriously as the Second Amendment to the United States Constitution.

By the first week of December, many families have already set up their Christmas trees complete with lights, tinsel, and ornaments. You can hear Christmas songs playing from Ida Sue's bakery, the grocery store, and pretty much every public establishment.

Even though I'm not a huge fan of Christmas, Greenwood Hospital is not exempt from the decorations. I figure that setting up the damn trees is less strenuous than having to tell every patient who asks why we haven't put up decorations that I'm not a fan of Christmas and watch as their faces fall in disappointment.

Before you think I'm a sadist, my parents weren't huge fans of the holiday either. We mostly spent Christmas traveling for Dad's work or waiting for him to come home from one of his special consultations because Mom hated spending Christmas without him.

So, unlike other normal kids, Anna and I rarely woke up to gifts under trees or stockings loaded with goodies. There's something different about this Christmas though. For the first time in a while, I may be spending it with someone I care about.

As I walk into the hospital, Lilian rushes up to me. "I've been texting and calling you."

"You have?" I ask, pulling out my phone to see that it's set to Do Not Disturb. "I must have mistakenly set it to DND. What's going on?"

"There's a couple here from Meadowville with their seven-year-old daughter to see you. Jolie says they've been here since eight am."

"Meadowville? That's like a two-hour drive from here. I don't remember making any such appointment."

"That's the thing, they don't have an appointment. They said they read an article you wrote online and they decided to come see you."

I stare at Lilian like a deer in headlights. "That's weird. Where are they?"

"They're waiting in the conference room."

"Alright. Let's not keep them waiting any longer."

We walk to the conference room and I can see a couple sitting down and holding hands. The usual worry lines I've come to associate with parents of chronically ill children are visible on their faces.

"Hi, I'm Dr. Levi Greenwood and this is my physician's assistant, Lilian Weatherby."

The man takes my extended hand. "I'm Owen Bernard, this is my wife Lucille, and that's our daughter Amelia."

"How may I be of help to you?" I say, taking a seat.

"We read one of your articles from a few years ago about a disease called MLD, and many of the symptoms you mentioned in that article are what we've been seeing with our Amelia. We decided to come see you, hoping that maybe you can help our little girl," Lucille sobs, and her husband rubs her back to comfort her.

Owen continues from where she stopped. "Amelia was a normal child, walking, running, talking, reading, and writing at her age level, but about six months ago, all that changed. Our vibrant baby girl couldn't make complete sentences anymore, she couldn't read or write, and soon even walking and sitting upright unassisted became a challenge for her."

"Plus, she has these very violent seizures that none of the seizure medications she's been given seem to alleviate. We've taken her to all the pediatricians in Meadowville but none of them have been able to tell us what's wrong with her. My baby girl can barely see anything anymore and yet no one can tell us what's wrong with her," Lucille chips in.

"We just want a diagnosis, Dr. Greenwood. How can anyone help her feel better when they don't even know what's wrong with her?"

I stand up and head over to Amelia, who's in a powered wheelchair. "Hi, Amelia. How are you doing? I'm Dr. Greenwood, and your mom and dad have told me all about you. How are you doing today?"

The little girl opens her mouth to speak, but she doesn't seem able to form sentences, and she isn't looking directly at me which means she may be partially blind.

"We'll need to run some tests on her, after which I'll consult with our resident neurologist and see if we can figure out what's going on. This may take a while, so you'll be admitted to the hospital. Hope that isn't a problem?"

"Not at all, Dr. Greenwood, whatever you say is best."

After the Bernards settle in, I call for Dr. Close and Dr. Thorne to consult on Amelia's case. After giving her a thorough physical examination, we send her for a CT scan, MRI, and EEG to study her brain wave patterns.

During her physical examination, which lasted about twenty minutes, she had two severe seizures. Just like her parents said, administering regular seizure medications did little to stop it.

"What do you think?" I ask Drs. Close and Thorne when we return to the conference room with her scans and test results.

"I've been a neurologist for five years and I've never had any patient who presented symptoms like hers before," Dr. Close says. "My first thought was that she may have a rare form of epilepsy, but I noticed some unusual rapid eye movements while we were examining her."

Dr. Thorne nods in agreement. "I noticed those too, but from the weakness in her limbs and muscles, it may be muscular dystrophy. Many patients with MD lose their motor functions over time just like Amelia has."

Dr. Close shakes his head. "I disagree. What about her vision problems? Her eye test results show that she's partially blind, and I'm certain that MD doesn't cause vision problems, let alone partial blindness."

"She may be suffering from MD and also having vision problems unrelated to it."

"And her seizures?"

"She may be epileptic."

"Not according to her EEG results," I cut in. "Her brain wave patterns are unlike anything I've ever seen with epilepsy before. I think I'm with Dr. Close on this one. Most epileptic seizures aren't quite as brutal as what we all just witnessed."

"What about MLD?" Lilian asks, and we all turn to stare at her. "Her parents mentioned an article you wrote about the disease and

I've been studying it. Most of the symptoms Amelia is presenting are typical of MLD."

"You're right, but metachromatic leukodystrophy is a very severe and rare condition. We need to eliminate the most common suspects first before we even start considering it, but thanks for your input," Dr Close tells her, and I nod in agreement.

Just then my phone beeps. It's a page from Amelia's room.

"It's Amelia. Dr. Close, come with me."

"I'm coming too," Dr. Thorne says, and we all race to her room together.

"What's going on?" I ask Jolie, putting on a pair of gloves.

"She's having another episode."

"How long since her last one?"

"Twelve minutes, eighteen seconds."

"They're getting closer," Dr. Close says.

"Yes. Get me ten milligrams of Midazolam stat."

Jolie hands me the injection and I wait till the seizure stops before administering it via her lap. In less than a minute, she goes completely still and her rapid breathing returns to normal.

We wait for about ten minutes to make sure she doesn't have another seizure. When I'm sure she's stable, I approach her parents who are pacing outside the room to give them an update.

"Her seizures are getting worse. From her EEG results, we noticed that there are some abnormal brain waves, but we've still not been able to determine why they're there."

Mr. Bernard sighs. "So it's not MLD?"

"It could be, but we can't be sure until we run a series of tests. Luckily I've been carrying out some research of my own so we have the equipment for genetic testing right here."

I see a gleam of hope flash in their eyes. "That's great, what about her seizures?"

"We decided to start her on one of the strongest anti-seizure meds, and it worked. Let's hope she doesn't have any negative reactions to it. The results of these genetic tests typically take three to four days to come out, so I suggest you take Amelia home and I'll contact you when the results are ready."

They hurry into their daughter's room and the rest of us—except for Dr. Thorne, who has been called for another case—go back to studying her charts and test results.

A few days later, Amelia's genetic test results reveal that there is no build-up of sulfatides in her nervous system, which is the main characteristic of MLD.

This takes us for a spin because, after days of in-depth research, we were almost sure that she has a variant of the disease and the test was supposed to confirm this.

"Is this the part where you tell us to take her somewhere else where they're better equipped to help her?" Amelia's mom asks when I tell her the test results. I can hear the heartbreak in her voice.

"No," I say, and Lilian looks up at me in shock. "My team and I will not rest until we find out what's wrong with Amelia."

"I thought we're not supposed to give our patients false hope?" she asks after I hang up.

"It's not false hope. You saw that young girl and how much she's suffering. We're not going to let her down. You, me, and Dr. Close are going to stay here as long as it takes till we find something that helps that little girl."

"Understood."

Lilian, Dr. Close, and I spend the next three days eating cafeteria food and scouring through every book in my office and every article online hoping to find something that sticks out.

"I think I have something," Lilian says, jumping up in excitement and running over to my side of the desk.

"It says here that three years ago, a young girl in California was diagnosed with Batten disease. Just take a look at her symptoms."

Dr. Close and I read through the article and by the end, we're nodding along with every word. "Oh no, this sounds exactly like the story Amelia's parents told me the day I met them. Loss of vision, speech, ability to sit upright or walk. I need to call Mikey, he's a pediatric neurologist in California and he may have more information about this Batten disease."

After my call with Mike, the only thing left is to call Amelia's parents to bring her in so we can draw some blood for more genetic testing. As suspected, her results come out a few days later and she tests positive for Juvenile Batten Disease CLN3, leaving all of us devastated.

I call her parents to come back to the hospital and when I break the news to them, they both burst into tears.

"Believe it or not, these are happy tears. We're just so happy that what's wrong with our daughter finally has an accurate name and diagnosis," Owen says, pulling his wife closer.

"You understand that it's a degenerative condition that has no cure and will ultimately take Amelia's life?" Dr. Close asks, taken aback by their reaction.

They both agree with a nod and I continue, "The good news is that now that we know what's wrong, my team of pediatricians, eye specialists, and physical therapists can come up with a treatment plan to slow down the disease's progression and improve her quality of life.

With the right medication and support, Amelia could live into her early or even late twenties, although she'll gradually lose more of her functions as time goes on."

Mr. and Mrs. Bernard kiss their daughter's cheek passionately. "Did you hear that, Amelia? Dr. Greenwood is gonna make you feel much better."

Amelia manages a smile and when I look over at Lilian, tears are pouring down her face.

Chapter Seventeen

♥

Lilian

You know how they say that one thing can happen and change the course of your entire life? Well, I never knew Amelia Bernard coming into Greenwood Hospital would be that one thing for me.

To think that when she was brought in, she was going to die in less than six months without a diagnosis. Now, with the proper treatment and care plan, her parents will get to have more time with her, which is amazing.

In our profession, what we mainly consider winning is helping patients discover and get rid of whatever is wrong with them so they can be healthy again. But then there are cases like Amelia's where winning could just be helping a parent put a name to what's wrong with their child.

Amelia's case is one that shakes everyone in the hospital to the core, including Jolie who says she'd never seen anyone endure the type of violent seizures Amelia's little body experienced in the few days she stayed with us.

Most of the other doctors and nurses had also never seen or heard of such a disease before, so everyone is highly invested in this case. And although the outcome breaks our hearts, it's great to watch her parents cry for joy at finally finding out what's wrong with their little girl.

As she comes in week after week to get her treatments, I'm reminded of how important what we do is, and how it can change people's lives in a heartbeat.

Now, I know in my heart that I can never leave the medical profession. I love music and I know music changes lives and gives people hope, but nothing will ever come close to the feeling of changing someone's life or giving them hope in this manner.

The only thing left for me to decide is in what capacity I continue to help people.

Notwithstanding Amelia's heartbreaking case, the Christmas cheer in the hospital is highly contagious. Donations of trees and decorations are pouring in from the townsfolk, while some have volunteered to come in and help decorate them.

Jolie, Laura, and I have been tasked with organizing the office Christmas party for the year and we meet during our lunch break to discuss what we want to do.

"I think we should do a Secret Santa this year. Each person in the hospital will randomly pick another person and buy a gift that's worth nothing more than twenty dollars for them," Laura suggests, grinning like she's just found the cure to cancer.

"Hmmm," Jolie grunts. "What if I don't like my gift, or my Secret Santa buys me something useless like oven mitts?"

Laura looks at her as if she's just said she has an incurable disease. "You don't like oven mitts?"

"I already have eight pairs."

"Oh," Laura says, smiling with relief. "For my Secret Santa, I choose Dr. Greenwood. I'd love to get him a gift that shows him how much I admire him."

There's this look in Laura's eyes that makes me suspect she's going to put a pair of her sexiest lingerie in Levi's gift box if we let her be his Secret Santa, and a twinge of jealousy zaps through my insides at the thought.

"Laura, you've been trying for years to get Dr. Greenwood to notice you and he hasn't. Honey, give it up already," Jolie chides her. I swear I feel the sudden urge to kiss her supple cheeks except I'd probably lose my lips if I tried that. "Lilian is his physician's assistant, she gets to be his Secret Santa. And you, Laura, will be Dr. Thorne's."

"Oh no! She never likes my gifts."

"You just have to put in a little extra effort in picking out her gift this time around. As for everyone else, I'll assign them to their Secret Santas."

If I hadn't been here when Laura came up with this Secret Santa idea, I'd have thought it was Jolie's with the way she took over. From the look on Laura's face, she's not happy about it either, but neither of us says anything in protest.

***

"Who are you texting that has you smiling like you just won the lottery?" Aiden asks, sitting beside me on the sofa.

"No one," I say, quickly hiding away my phone.

"I don't believe you. I've been watching you engrossed in that phone, exchanging texts and smiling from ear to ear. Are you seeing someone?"

"Don't be ridiculous. What time do I have to date someone when I spend all of it in the hospital?"

"None, unless you're taking a leaf from a character in *Grey's Anatomy* and getting hot and heavy with someone at the hospital."

"Grow up, Aiden, no one in real hospitals hooks up the way they do on that show," I say, heading to the refrigerator to grab a bottle of water.

"Then why are you acting all weird and turning red? I'm right, aren't I?"

"Why don't you focus on your love life and get your nose out of my nonexistent one."

"Maybe I'll ask Levi, I bet he'll know who it is."

"Okay fine. You're right, I met someone," I blurt out in a panic.

"I knew it. Who is he and where did you guys meet?"

"I'm not gonna tell you who he is. I like him a lot and I don't wanna jinx it. We met at The Sunshine Café last month."

"That's great, I hope it works out. So, you're gonna spend Christmas with us right? You don't have a night shift that day or something?"

"Mom sent you to come do her dirty work huh?"

He smiles and puts a hand on my shoulder. "You know me too well."

As I drive to work later that evening, I realize that despite my not wanting Aiden to know about Levi and me, there's another reason I didn't tell him. It's because there's nothing to tell, not really.

Yes, Levi and I may be attracted to each other. We may have had a mind-blowing lovemaking session in the park and exchanged flirty texts here and there, but we've never really defined our relationship.

From watching *He's Just Not That Into You* about a million times, I'm a firm believer in not jumping to conclusions about dating a guy unless he explicitly says he wants to date you.

Are Levi and I just two people attracted to each other who kiss and have sex on occasion, or are we colleagues with benefits?

Staying in the dark about where I stand with someone, especially when we're bumping ugliest, isn't one of my strong suits. So, as I pull into an empty parking space, I'm determined not to let today end without knowing exactly where I stand with him.

The only challenge now is how to bring up the conversation in a completely normal way without looking or sounding desperate.

"Lilian, you're with me. We're making a house call," Levi says when we run into each other in the lobby.

"Really?" I ask him, almost jumping for joy at the golden opportunity the universe has gifted me.

"Yes. As you know, Lucy Bunch's father has an inoperable brain tumor and I'm part of the team managing his end-of-life care. Yesterday they called and said that he's been having seizures, so we have to go find out what could be the cause and figure out how to alleviate it," he explains as we drive out of the parking lot.

"Oh, that's too bad."

"Yeah, he used to be such a vibrant and active man. You should have seen him train the horses or take the cattle to pasture. Even at seventy-nine he was such a beast, but unfortunately, brain tumors don't care about that."

Soon we arrive at Lucy Bunch's ranch, and the place is as large and as busy as I remember. Lucy, who's by the stables, waves us over and after exchanging pleasantries we proceed into the main house.

I notice how much older and grayer she looks since the last time I saw her. I guess losing a husband, being on the verge of losing a father, and managing such a huge ranch single-handedly will do that to you.

We spend about an hour with the old man and Levi conducts a thorough physical examination before adjusting his medication to manage the seizures.

On our way back to the hospital, I keep thinking of a casual way to slip what has been on my mind into our chit-chat. Maybe the reason I'm finding it this hard to talk to Levi isn't only that I don't want him to see me as desperate. I'm also kinda scared about what his response will be.

What if he just wants us to be casual? The thought of him saying that fills me with dread, but it's better to find out now than later.

"So... Aiden asked me if I was seeing someone this morning."

He's silent for a few seconds which feels like an eternity. "And what did you tell him?"

"Quite frankly, even if I wanted to, I didn't know what to tell him. Mostly because we haven't defined what we are, and I've learned from experience that you need to define relationships explicitly."

He smiles and takes my hand in his, our fingers interlocking with each other's. "Lily, I like you. I like you a lot."

"Um, I like pizza a lot so that doesn't clear things up for me."

He slows down and eventually parks the car by the side of the road. "I'm sure I like you a little more than you like pizza."

"You don't know how much I like pizza."

"Do you like it so much that you can't wait to see it every day, that you dream about it almost every night?"

"Maybe not that much. But look, the reason I'm asking this is because I've been here before. I liked this guy a lot and I thought we were on the same page with our relationship. Turned out he was going on dates with other people and toying with my feelings all along. I need to know that's not what's happening here."

He lifts my face with his fingers till I'm looking into his eyes. "I would never toy with you or your feelings. I like you, I'm eager to see where our relationship is headed and I am certainly not going on other dates."

"Except the date with Nancy Taylor?"

"Aiden didn't tell you how that date ended, did he?"

"I never asked, I didn't want to seem too interested."

"Then let me tell you how it went. I intentionally came an hour late to the restaurant and then I spent about fifteen minutes telling her how horrible dating a doctor who will constantly put his job above her and never have time for her would be."

I cackle. "What?"

"It gets worse."

"No!"

"When she went to the bathroom to freshen up, I paid for our food and left without saying goodbye."

"Oh my gosh, that was horrible. Why would you do that?"

"I felt so bad for being on the date in the first place that I knew I had to sabotage it."

"And what did Aiden do?"

"Nothing. He just kept looking at me like I'd lost my damn mind. So, are you now convinced that we're on the same page?"

I lean toward him and kiss him till we're both struggling to catch our breath.

"Is that a good enough answer for you?" I ask when our lips finally come apart.

"I think that's the only way we should respond to each other's questions from now on."

"Let's get out of here."

Chapter Eighteen

Levi

The hospital Christmas party is finally here and I'm actually excited for it.

Unbelievable.

For the past few years, especially since Dad retired, I used to dread it. The singing, dancing, the trees, the lights. I hated all of it—except maybe the food, drinks, and pastries.

I tried to stop Christmas parties from happening after my dad left, but everyone in the hospital almost bit my head off and I never mentioned it again.

I didn't miss the surprised look on Jolie's face when I thanked her after she told me I was Lilian's Secret Santa instead of rolling my eyes like I always used to when she mentioned anything about Christmas.

Nor the shock on Phil's face when I threw him a "Good job on the tree decorations" on my way out of the hospital last week.

This morning as I walk into the break room to speak with Dr. Thorne, I hear some of the nurses gossiping about how they're going to spend Christmas. The moment I appear in the doorway, all talk ceases and everyone stares at me like the Grinch has just made an appearance.

"Merry almost Christmas, everyone."

They're so shocked that no one responds to my greeting, so I ask Dr. Thorne if I can speak with her.

"Were you trying to be sarcastic just then?" she asks, leaning on the wall beside us.

"No, that was genuine."

She raises her brows at me suspiciously. "Since when?"

I shrug. "Since I realized I've been wetting everyone's festive blanket."

She heaved a sigh of relief. "Oh, thank God. You hating Christmas like your dad was weird. So what did you want?"

"We got this new case today and I believe it's right up your alley. I want you to go check out the patient and get back to me with your findings."

"What room is the patient?"

"First floor, two rooms to your right."

"Alright, you got it."

"Good morning, Dr. Greenwood," Lilian greets when I get to my office.

"Hi, Ms. Weatherby."

After I shut the door behind me, I pull her close to me and bury my nose in the crook of her neck. "You smell really good today, new perfume?"

"Yeah, I'm trying something new."

"It suits you."

"Thanks. So, I'm sure you already know that I'm your Secret Santa. I know you're mine and I just wanted to let you know that if you don't get me anything, it's fine."

I raise my face to look at her. "Oh no, you too?"

"Yeah. Laura told me all about how much you hate this holiday."

"There goes my hope that at least one person here doesn't know what a grinch I am."

"It's okay, I kinda thought the Grinch was adorable."

"No, you didn't. You're just saying that to make me feel less shitty."

She laughs. "Maybe a little bit, but seriously though, I wasn't a fan of Christmas either."

"What eventually changed your mind?"

"My time in New York made me understand the true essence of Christmas and why people love it so much. It isn't about Santa Claus or the gifts or the delicious cookies, it's about family. This holiday is the only time many people get to see all the members of their family together under one roof. I realized how much I missed my family on those few Christmases I spent without them."

I pick up my tablet. "That's probably why it sucks for me. We hardly ever spent Christmas as a family while I was growing up and even less now that I'm an adult. With Mom gone, Anna in Chicago with her family, and my dad—the OG Grinch—it just seems like a formality at this point."

"Maybe one day you'll have your own family and start your own Christmas traditions with them."

I stare unwaveringly into her eyes. "Maybe."

"Till then, I can convince Aiden to invite you to spend the day with us at the Weatherby mansion, visitors are always welcome."

"Actually, Aiden and I have this tradition of going fishing on the twenty-fifth just to spite the holiday, and we're all set for this year's spite fishing trip. I had no idea that I'd find someone worth spending the day with."

"You're sweet, but it's okay. We still have the Christmas party tonight and I'm pretty sure you'll love your gift. Just don't open it in public."

"Okay, now I'm officially excited for Christmas," I say as we leave my office to commence ward rounds.

***

At around eight pm, almost everyone is in the staff lounge for the party. Many of the staff who are off duty have changed into their party wear and those who are on duty remain in their scrubs.

A few of our patients and the family members caring for them are also present.

As hospital staff and patients mingle with each other, Mariah Carey's 1994 classic "All I Want for Christmas Is You" starts playing in the background just as Lilian walks into the room.

She's wearing a red gown per the theme of the night and I'm amazed at how she still manages to stand out amid all the red currently dominating the room.

Suddenly, it hits me that at this moment, Mariah Carey is right. All I want for Christmas is this gorgeous woman who has unlocked a part of me I was starting to believe no longer functioned—my heart.

As she catches my gaze from across the room, we share a secret smile before Phil approaches her and offers her a drink.

Despite Laura yapping my ears off about something she seems passionate about, I don't hear two words she says because I spend half the time following Lilian with my eyes.

When she and Phil get on the dance floor, my blood begins boiling so hard that I feel like walking straight to them and telling him and everyone else in the room that she's mine. Rather than do that, I hit my wine glass with my car keys, drawing everyone's attention to me.

"I just want to use this moment to thank every one of you for your hard work and dedication to this hospital and our patients. Since I took charge of the hospital one year ago now, you all have made the transition very easy for me and I want to thank you for that. My dad hardly spoke highly of anything or anyone, as you all know, but he always spoke so highly of you and I have seen why. As for our wonderful patients and their families who have joined us today, thanks for choosing Greenwood Hospital and we promise to keep giving you all the best treatment possible."

Jolie walks up to me and whispers something in my ear.

"And I've just been told that it's time to exchange gifts. Cheers and Merry Christmas everyone."

"Merry Christmas," they all echo, and sounds of glasses clinking against each other fill the room.

As most people exchange gifts with their Secret Santas, Lilian approaches me and hands me a small box. "Remember, open only when you're alone."

I pick up a wrapped box from underneath the tree and hand it to her. "And here's my present to you."

"Did you just steal a gift from under the tree?"

"Of course not, I bought and wrapped this myself. Okay, maybe not the wrapping part but I picked out the gift myself."

She gives it a little shake. "It sounds expensive. I hope you obeyed the twenty-dollar limit rule?"

"I've never been one to obey rules, so no."

"This was very thoughtful, thank you," she says, rewarding me with a smile that never fails to take my breath away.

"You're welcome."

Impatient to open her gift, I sneak away to the restroom and when I open the box, I gasp.

Inside the box is a pair of sexy red panties and a note that reads: *To remind you of me till next time.*

All the blood in my brain rushes down to my cock, leaving it hard as a brick wall.

When I go back into the staff lounge, I find a way to slip Lilian a note of my own and I watch her till she finds a moment to open it.

She blushes and looks up to find my eyes on her and she bites her lips, smiles, and looks away.

My note reads: *I love the lingerie but PS: I don't need reminders of how much I want to ravish you, the hardness in my briefs every time I'm around you is enough reminder.*

***

Four days later, on the twenty-fifth, Levi and I drive to the fishing dock. Dad was particularly cranky this morning and insisted I take down the Christmas lights in the house as they were blinding him.

His younger sister, my Aunt Debbie, came around to visit and decided to put up some decorations despite all my warnings not to. So when Dad started acting up, I left her to deal with him.

"The whole town looks like we're driving through the North Pole. I don't get all this obsession over a freaking holiday. I think we may be the last sane people left in this town."

"Maybe not. A few days ago, someone explained it to me in a way that made sense."

Aiden stares at me, eyes wide with disbelief. "Please don't tell me you've caught the Christmas bug. I can't lose you too."

"Take it easy. It's not like I'm planning to put on a Santa costume or hit the streets to knock on people's doors and sing carols for them. I'm just saying that I now get why so many people are obsessed with the holiday."

"This will be good. Alright, Christmas guru, enlighten me."

"Remember that the words I'm about to say are not mine, I'm simply quoting what someone told me. For many people, Christmas isn't about the trees, decorations, or gifts. It's about family and a rare opportunity to spend time with them under the same roof."

Aiden shrugs. "I guess I'll never get the novelty in that, since I practically have all my family members living under the same roof already."

"Hmm, if you think about it, every day is like Christmas for you."

"Fuck! You're right. Thank you for ruining the remainder of my time in that house."

"What are friends for?" I say in a sarcastic tone.

Thirty minutes later, we arrive at the dock, take out our fishing equipment from Aiden's trunk, and get ready to start fishing.

After connecting the line to the rod and reel, we secure the worms we use as bait to the hook before lowering it into the calm water. We then sit by the edge of the dock, our legs dangling above the water.

"So, Nancy has been asking for your number nonstop," Aiden says after we settle down.

"You're kidding, right?"

"I wish. Apparently, she likes guys who seem unavailable. She said something about liking the chase."

"She actually used those words?"

"Yep."

"What is she, a predator?"

"Which makes you her prey," Aiden says, letting out a hearty laugh.

"It's great that one of us finds this amusing."

Aiden's rod vibrates and he hurriedly pulls it up, believing he's caught a fish, but the hook comes up empty. Disappointed, he releases it back into the water.

"What's wrong with you anyway?"

"What do you mean?"

"I've never known you to turn a smoking hot girl like Nancy down before. If I remember correctly, since you broke up with Stella, you tend to prefer women who don't want commitment."

I sigh. "I'm almost thirty-eight years old, man. I think maybe it's time to find a nice girl to start a serious relationship with, maybe even settle down."

"Oh my God! I knew it."

"Knew what?"

"That you're seeing someone. There are only two things that make a man talk the way you are. It's either you're seeing someone and it's serious, serious enough that you two or one of you has said the L word, *or* you're burning up your sheets with some hottie."

"Please don't say hottie."

"So there is a hottie?"

Aiden *would throw up if he knew it's his sister he's calling "some hottie."*

"There's no one. I was just thinking out loud, not talking to a ten-year-old. How's your girlfriend by the way? She doesn't mind that you're spending today fishing with your buddy instead of with her?"

"Nah. Maureen and I get each other, that's why we work."

"You seem to like her."

He nods affirmatively. "I do, and it's been a while since I felt this way about someone, but you probably know what I mean."

"No clue."

He laughs. "As long as my sister isn't the one you're knocking boots with, I'm happy for you either way."

Just then my rod and line start shaking violently and I reel it in to see a huge fish caught on the hook.

"That's what I'm talking about!" Aiden yells excitedly.

Thank you, fish. Your timing couldn't have been more perfect.

Chapter Nineteen

♥

Lilian

Finally, the festive season is over and everything has returned to normal in Elvesridge.

The streets and homes previously covered in Christmas lights and ornaments now lay bare, everyone looking forward and being optimistic about what the new year has in store for them.

With the preparation for our town's first-ever singing competition and animal adoption underway, Levi and I have been busier than bees.

Fliers for the auditions—both virtual and physical—have been put up everywhere, and tickets are available for sale at the local café, grocery store, and other small businesses around town.

When Aiden and Maureen—who are also animal lovers like us—found out the main reason why we're hosting the competition, they asked to join our team.

We speak to the mayor and town council members, and after explaining the reason for the competition, they throw their weight behind us.

Since it's the first time such a competition has ever been hosted in Elvesridge, a lot of people have been skeptical about its success and some are excited about it.

But none of that deters us from recruiting more young people to help put up more fliers and spread the word all over town.

Elvesridge High—our alma mater—has graciously allowed us to use the school auditorium for our auditions, rehearsals, and the competition itself, so everything is almost set for D-day which is in two weeks.

When Levi and I walk into the school grounds on the first day of auditions, it feels like a dead zone.

Levi looks around. "Where is everyone? They saw the fifty thousand dollar grand prize on the flier, right?"

"The feedback I've gotten is that people's reactions to the fliers have not been very encouraging. Having the auditions at 6 pm couldn't have helped either. I mean who would show up for an unpopular show's audition this late in the evening?" I ask as we walk toward the school's auditorium.

"Well, if we don't see anyone, we'll come back and keep coming back until people start showing up."

As we push open the auditorium door, our jaws drop in shock to see that the three-hundred-seater auditorium is almost half filled with people.

"We were saying?" Levi asks, holding the door open for me to go in.

"Are you sure they know what's happening here, or are they here for something else?"

"There's only one way to find out."

He climbs the stage and claps to get the crowd's attention.

"Hello! Can I have everyone's attention, please? My partner Lilian and I booked this auditorium ahead of tonight to hold the auditions for the singing competition. If that's not the reason you are here, please feel free to leave us."

We wait for a few minutes but no one makes any attempt to leave so we proceed with the auditions.

We hadn't put any age limits on the flier so everyone from smaller kids to senior citizens are here. Even Diana Fallon, a lady who is almost eighty years old, is here to audition. When she sings, she blows us away with her voice and earns herself a spot among the final fifteen contestants.

"I never knew Elvesridge had such amazing singers, did you?" I ask Levi after Priscilla Wembley, the mayor's daughter, auditions.

"I had no clue."

Despite Levi's announcement, some people who don't have any business being here still get up to audition. I lose count of how many times we have to stop someone to remind them that we are having auditions for a singing competition, not a dance or karate competition.

After about two hours of auditions, it's difficult but we manage to cut down the singers to our top fifteen contestants. Out of these fifteen, the final ten who will be part of the main competition will be selected after the next round.

However, auditions are not the only thing we're doing to get ready for the competition. As we get the singers ready, we also get the dogs ready with the help of a dog and cat trainer Levi hired.

They are to teach the dogs and cats a few simple tricks that they'll perform on the day of the competition—because what's cuter than dogs and cats with big brown eyes? Dogs and cats with big brown eyes who do tricks.

By the time we're done, the people of Elvesridge won't know what hit them.

As the day of the competition draws closer, the buzz both online and off is growing massively. With four days left until the competition, tickets to attend the show have sold out.

Many people start calling in to express their desire to attend even with the school auditorium capacity maxed out. After much deliberation, we decide that the best thing to do would be to change venues, since our goal is to get as many people as possible to come for the show so that the chances of the animals getting adopted will increase significantly.

The only other place in town that can accommodate such a crowd is the local park. Since the weather in Houston is typically warm in January, we can have events outdoors without freezing temperatures. We contact the park authority and get all the necessary permits from them to use the park for the event.

Using the park is going to cost us a lot more than we budgeted, but with the donations pouring in from everyone and Levi's benevolence, we know we can pull it off. When he said he would take care of the financial aspect of the competition, I didn't understand how much he meant it till now.

He's asked that most of the donations that people are sending in be set aside for Pete and The Four-legged Haven, while he provides the bulk of the money we're using to purchase the supplies needed for the show.

Neil Morgan, who is still grateful for how we handled his daughter when she came in with bleach poisoning, offers to support our cause with a huge donation.

He requests that his donation be used to increase the grand prize for the winner of the competition from fifty to a hundred thousand dollars.

Ida Sue's bakery offers to make all the snacks we need to entertain everyone in attendance, for a much smaller fee than we would've paid.

In addition to the donations of both money and other items, people have also donated their time to help us set up for the competition. All we have to do is provide refreshments for them to refuel during our short breaks.

We spend the whole of the night before the competition building the stage and stage lights, and when at last the day of the competition arrives, we spend the morning setting up the sound systems and putting up the seating arrangements.

An hour to the time, Aiden, Maureen, Levi and I rush home to freshen up and come back before people start arriving.

At three pm, the show commences, and we start with the treat we've been planning for the people. Levi and I are going to sing "Don't Go Breaking My Heart" by Elton John and Kiki Dee.

Everyone, including Aiden, is confused when we make the announcement but by the end of our rendition, the crowd is on their feet cheering and clapping so loudly I can barely hear myself breathe.

Next, the contestants begin their performances with the songs Levi and I chose for them. We chose songs that best suited their voices to give everyone a fair chance of winning.

After the first round of performances, five singers are eliminated and five are left for the final round.

"Hello, Elvesridge! How are you all doing tonight?" Pete asks after he takes the stage. "Many of you may know me as the owner of The Four-Legged Haven, and others know me as just Pete, but what many of you may not know is that The Four-Legged Haven is about to close down. We have some of the cutest and most intelligent animals in the shelter and they're at risk of getting put down or sent away if new homes aren't found for them. I therefore urge you all to please adopt a pet today. Let's give it up for a little demonstration by our four-legged furry friends."

The crowd watches in awe as the dogs take the stage, doing tricks such as shaking the trainer's hands, rolling over on their backs on command, and giving high fives to the trainer and each other. The crowd goes wild with every silly trick they perform.

The cats take the stage after them and although they do fewer tricks than the dogs, it's still pretty fun to watch. One of the cats refuses to do any of the tricks, she just sits there and watches everyone, which has the audience hollering. Afterward, she walks off majestically and crawls onto the mayor's lap.

"I guess I have a cat now," he says, and the crowd ripples in laughter.

After the animal tricks, the singing competition continues and eventually, we come down to our last two singers. Priscilla Wembley and Amy, an eleven-year-old girl.

The judges let the audience decide which of them will take the crown, and after their final performances, the people choose Amy as their winner.

After presenting her with her check for a hundred thousand dollars and a consolation prize for Priscilla, we urge everyone to walk around and adopt a pet.

Many people walk up to Levi and me to give us compliments about our wonderful voices, with many asking if we're a couple. Whenever we say no, they look crushed, and some tell us what a great couple we'd make.

"You know, I've never actually taken you out on a real date, and I want to," he says to me when the fuss around us eventually dies down. "Sunday night, you and I are going on a date."

"Oh yeah? I think people will notice us wining and dining in public, which will be funny since we just spent this entire evening trying to convince them that we're not a couple."

"Okay fine, I'll cook dinner for you at my place."

"You mean your chef will."

He shakes his head. "No, I mean I will."

"You cook?"

"Yeah, I do."

"Interesting. You're just a man of many mysterious layers aren't you?"

"You can say that again. Just get ready to eat the most delicious pasta you've ever had."

"What about your dad? Won't he freak out when he finds out that we're dating?"

"First of all, he's a guest in my house, and secondly, who I choose to date is none of his business."

"Okay then, that's great. It's a date."

By the end of the night, Pete gives us the great news that all the animals have been adopted, and with the money we raised he can keep the shelter open and keep helping other animals that need it.

We're all very happy that our efforts were not in vain and we achieved what we set out to achieve.

Chapter Twenty

♥

Levi

"Dad, I'm having someone over for dinner tonight so please, I need you to behave."

"What do you mean by behave?"

"Well, I need you to be cordial and nice to her in case you two see each other at any point."

He shoots me a glare. "When have I ever been rude to your guests?"

"You told Stella she wasn't good enough for me the first time you met her," I reply, rinsing off the shaving stick.

"But I was right, wasn't I? She left you a day before your wedding."

"Dad, that's not the point. The point is I really like this new person and I don't want you to do anything to screw it up for me okay?"

"Fine. I'll stay in my room and stay out of your way."

"That will be great. Also, try not to provoke Nurse Kayla 'cause if she leaves, I'm calling you know who."

"You wouldn't dare."

"I would," I say, staring him down.

"Aren't you supposed to be focused on your career and running the hospital right now instead of dating anyway?"

"I'm a grown man. I think I can navigate running a hospital and dating at the same time."

"Whatever," he grunts.

By seven pm—an hour before Lilian's arrival—I make sure that Dad is good and has all he needs to sustain him till tomorrow morning.

I also send all the staff home for the night except for Nurse Kayla who I've given detailed instructions on how to care for Dad.

A few minutes past eight, the doorbell rings, and when I open the door, Lilian is standing there looking breathtaking in a blue dress with a thigh-high slit and her golden hair flowing down her neck.

"Are you going to invite me in?" she asks, and I realize I've been so busy gawking at her that I've forgotten my manners.

"Please come in."

When she walks into the living room, I kiss her and take off her jacket which I hang on the coat rack near the door.

"You have a very beautiful home," she says, looking around in amazement.

"Did you think I lived in a bachelor pad?"

"Kinda," she says, and we both laugh.

"Well, you're in for more surprises tonight."

"Good ones I hope?"

"Great ones."

I lead her to the kitchen, pour her a glass of wine, and throw on my apron to commence cooking.

"Oh wow, I've never watched a guy prepare dinner for me before. I have to say, it's really sexy."

"Wait till you taste it then, you'll be begging me to become your personal chef."

She stands up and walks toward me. "Can I help you, or am I not allowed in your kitchen?"

"I thought you'd never ask," I say, helping her put on her apron.

Standing this close to her, her body rubbing against mine as I fasten the apron, I'm tempted to lower my lips to kiss her neck and breathe in her intoxicating scent. But, I promised her a home-cooked meal and a gentleman keeps his promises.

By now, the water I set on the stove is boiling so I pour the pasta into it.

"You're gonna help me stir the pasta while I prepare the sauce," I tell her, handing her a long spoon.

"So where did you learn to cook?" she asks as she stirs the pasta gently.

"When we were younger, my mom was a great cook and she always made me stay with her in the kitchen when she cooked. I hated it because all I wanted to do was play with my friends and watch TV. But as I grew older, knowing how to cook came in handy and I appreciated her for making me learn."

"That's great. You must miss your mom huh?"

"Yeah, my mom was the sweetest when I was a kid, but as we grew, her alcohol addiction changed her into someone I didn't recognize a lot of the time. After she died, though, I missed her more than I thought I would."

"I'm so sorry."

I shrug. "Nothing to be sorry about, shit happens. How about you, where did you learn to cook?"

"Oh, because I offered to help you cook, you think I can? I'm just glad you told me to stir some pasta. Anything else and the fire department would be paying you a visit tonight."

"Oh thank God 'cause I almost asked you to make the sauce," I joke, and she flashes a smile my way.

Soon the pasta is all done and I dish it into two plates before we sit to enjoy our dinner.

"Oh my God! You weren't kidding," she moans. The sound takes me back to our night in the park. "Levi, this is the best pasta I've ever had and I mean that."

"I'm glad you like it."

"It's so good. You know, it amazes me how you're this phenomenal neurosurgeon, have the singing voice of an angel, and now it just so happens that you're a great cook. More people need to know how great you are, truly."

"You mean I need to show people I'm more than just a hard-ass? No thanks," I say, and we both share a laugh.

After we finish our dinner, I ask her to come to the kitchen with me for some dessert. As I feed her the first spoon of ice cream cake, she closes her eyes to savor the taste. When she opens them, my face is a few inches away from hers.

I raise my hand to the scar in between her lashes and gently trace it with my index finger. "How did you get that?"

She swallows. "I think it was when I fell off my bike as a kid."

"It's beautiful...you're beautiful and I want to kiss you so badly," I say, my voice almost a whisper.

"You have no idea how much I was hoping you'd say that."

I place my hands behind her head and pull her face closer till our lips meet, our eyes fluttering closed as we savor each other's sweetness.

Our last time was a bit rushed, so I intend to take it slow this time around and cherish each moment. I gently ease my tongue into her mouth and hers is right there, eager to meet mine, as we twirl around in each other's mouth. Despite having kissed her many times, I still can't seem to get enough of her lips, enough of her tongue coated with the sweet aftertaste of the ice cream cake.

I finally pull my mouth away from hers, the soft skin of her neck inviting me to suck on it, which I do. Not like I have a choice—I need to taste all of her.

As I trail kisses down her neck, she throws her head back and moans, her fingers grabbing a fistful of my hair.

"I want to see you...all of you," I whisper to her when my lips find her ear.

"Take me to your bedroom then," she says, and I sweep her up in my arms, half running and half walking up the stairs.

When we get to the bedroom, I put her down gently, my arms going around her back to unzip her blue dress. She shrugs it off and I watch as it slides over her hips before pooling at her feet.

She steps out of it and unhooks her bra, a gasp escaping my throat as I see her bare breasts in the moonlit room. They're as gorgeous as I remember, even more gorgeous now that I've seen them without any restrictions.

I start to cross over to her but she shakes her head no. "Your turn, I want to see you too."

Taking off my shirt, I throw it on the ground and unzip my fly before stepping out of my pants.

"The briefs too," she says, her voice thick with lust and desire.

I watch her face as I pull down my briefs. The moment my erection springs out, her eyes widen in pleasure.

I close the space between us and when our naked and warm bodies meet, I feel shock waves run across my entire length.

She traces her fingers across my chest, down my torso. Then lower and lower till her fist is wrapped around my throbbing length.

"Lily," I moan. "I want to taste you."

Without waiting for a response, I gently push her down on the bed and take off her panties, my breath catching in my throat when I part her legs to see her pussy, pink and swollen, waiting to be ravished.

I trail kisses down her thighs until I get to the intersection between them. By now, she's squirming, her thighs trembling in anticipation as she awaits my next move. I part her pussy lips to reveal her swollen nub and lower my head down to her pussy, my tongue flicking over her clit.

"Oh fuck," she moans when I take her clit into my mouth, sucking, licking, and blowing at intervals.

She tastes like I imagined she would, like a woman wild with desire, inching closer and closer to her untethered release.

As her moans increase and her hands in my hair grip tighter, I know she's close to cumming on my face so I speed up my licking. She's shivering now, her thighs squeezing my head, but I don't stop. I won't stop until she cries out my name in sweet release.

And I don't have to wait too long because suddenly she stops moving.

"Oh, Levi!" she cries out, her entire body shaking as she comes apart with the pleasure of her intense orgasm.

I watch her, completely in awe of how beautiful she looks at this moment, her eyes rolling back into her head and the biggest smile plastered on her face.

I crawl on top of her and lower my lips to her breasts, taking her nipples into my mouth and rolling them with my lips.

She moans and grabs my rock-hard erection. "I want you inside me," she says, a wild look in her eyes that I've not seen all night.

I open the drawer on my nightstand and take out a pack of condoms, tearing one packet open with my teeth and rolling it over my cock. Looking into her big brown eyes, I slowly ease myself into her, moaning as my arousal slides into her wetness.

She feels warm and incredible as I drive myself slowly into her, increasing my pace with every thrust. She lifts herself to meet my thrusts, our hips grinding into each other in a steady rhythm.

As I feel the pressure rise in my cock, I slow down and lower my lips to hers, unwilling to cum just yet.

I lower my lips until they find her nipples again and I resume my thrusts. This time, they are hard and fast and unyielding.

She grabs onto my back, her nails digging into my flesh as I drive us both to where we've been desperate to get to.

"Oh fuck, Lily..." I groan, unable to stop myself as spurts of my seed splash into the condom.

At the same moment, her body begins to shudder under mine as her second orgasm hits her, our ecstatic moans filling the silence of the room.

Chapter Twenty-One

♥

Lilian

Ever since Amelia's case, the workload at Greenwood Hospital has tripled.

YouTuber Warren Berkeley, famous for sharing touching stories like Amelia's, caught wind of Amelia's story after the local news interviewed her parents. He then came down from New Hampshire to Meadowville to do a more in-depth interview with the Bernards.

In this interview, the Bernards mentioned and acknowledged Levi, Greenwood Hospital, and the staff for our help. Since the interview was posted on Warren's almost ten-million subscriber channel, we've been getting calls, messages, and patients from different corners of the country.

Many days, we're so busy that there isn't time to take a break or have lunch. I don't even get to have shifts anymore because as Levi's physicians assistant, I need to be by his side to handle the buttload of cases that are coming his way.

"I think we need to hire more doctors and nurses, the workload has become a bit unbearable the past few weeks," I say as we come out from our third spinal fusion surgery of the day and head to the consultation room to see some new patients.

Levi nods in agreement. "I think you're right. I'll tell HR to get on that immediately."

"This may not be the right time to bring this up again, but I think it's high time you heard the ideas I have that can help the hospital and staff perform more efficiently. Last time I brought it up, you shut me down, but I—"

"I'm sorry about that, I was a jerk, but I promise I want to hear your ideas by the end of the shift or whenever we catch a break," he says as we walk into the consulting room.

I open a patient file on the iPad. "Our next patient has a growth on her knee she wants you to check out."

"These patients realize I'm a neurosurgeon, not an orthopedic surgeon right?"

"I don't think they do, which is why we need to update your profile and that of the other doctors on the hospital's website. That thing was last updated like five years ago," I say, stepping out to bring in our next patient.

We spend the next few hours seeing patients and referring the ones whose cases aren't neurologically related to the appropriate doctors.

By the time we're done seeing patients, plus some emergency case interruptions, it's past eight pm and I'm so exhausted that I decide to take a nap in the on-call room before heading home.

When I wake up, Laura is sitting on the bed beside mine munching on the last piece of a Snickers bar.

"Hey, Laura, what's the time?"

"Last I checked, it was quarter to ten."

"Oh wow, I had an exhausting shift today."

Laura tilts her head as she studies me. "You don't look it, you're glowing. I noticed this morning but I was too preoccupied to tell you. It's unfair that every other person looks homeless and you're glowing."

"Oh stop it, it's probably because I took a nap. I'll see you tomorrow."

"Good night, Lil."

Fifteen minutes later, I get home and collapse into bed without eating dinner. By midnight, hunger pangs have me awake and paying the refrigerator a visit for a midnight snack.

I make myself some warm milk, pairing it with some crackers and cheese. As I sit down to enjoy my snack, I hear footsteps approaching and it turns out to be Mom, which I'm not feeling great about. Our encounters always lead to a lecture of some kind and I'm not in the mood for that right now.

"What are you doing down here at this ungodly hour? I thought thieves had broken into the house or something."

That's when I look at her hands and see she has a handgun. "Jesus, Mom, what were you gonna do with that?"

"Show the burglar he picked the wrong house to rob." She looks at my crackers and warm milk. "You shouldn't eat this late at night, it's not healthy and it seems you're gaining a little bit of weight."

I roll my eyes at her. "Do you think you can interact with me for more than a minute without finding a way to sneak an insult in there somehow? When I came home I was too skinny, and now I'm gaining some weight."

"What? I didn't insult you either time, I was simply stating my observation, or am I not allowed to do that?"

"You can do whatever you want, I'm going to bed and I'm taking these with me," I say, grabbing my glass of milk and the remaining crackers.

"Good night," she calls after me.

I mutter "whatever" under my breath as I head back to my room.

Despite my late-night sleep disruption, I'm up early the next morning, getting ready to leave for the hospital.

As I lift my otherwise flat eyelashes with some mascara, I catch my reflection in the full-length mirror in front of me.

Maybe Mom was right, my breasts look a bit bigger than usual. And now that I think about it, they've been a little tender to the touch lately.

I lift my scrubs and there's an almost unnoticeable pouch in my lower abdominal area. That's not abnormal, though. I'm usually bloated whenever my period is around the corner and sometimes my boobs hurt.

Wait a minute, what's today's date? I open the calendar app on my phone. *That can't be right.*

If today is the twenty-eighth, that means that I'm a few days shy of being four weeks late to see my period. Have I been so busy at the hospital that I didn't realize I hadn't seen my period for almost a month?

I mean, my period has never been one to follow a tight schedule, I've been late in the past, but never this late.

"Don't freak out, don't freak out," I tell myself as I quickly go back one month to check my calendar where I tick off each day after taking my birth control pill.

I scroll to the day of the meteor shower and to my great horror, it's unticked. I forgot to take my pill that day, and that was the night Levi and I took our relationship to the next level, without any protection whatsoever.

Oh shit! Okay, now I can freak out!

Just then I hear a soft knock on my door and Aiden walks into my room. "Lily, are you okay? Your hands are shaking."

"Just a little chilly is all."

"Really? It's a pretty warm day. Are you sure you're not coming down with something?"

"I'm practically a doctor, Aiden. I think I'd know if I'm coming down with something," I say, almost cackling at the irony of my statement. "Did you want something?"

"Oh yeah. My car is at the mechanic's getting serviced, so I was wondering if you could drop me off at the gym on your way to the hospital."

"Sure thing. I'll be out in a second."

When Aiden leaves my room, I take a deep breath and steady myself before heading downstairs to meet him.

"Are you sure you're okay? You don't seem like yourself," he says when we get in the car.

"I'm just stressed out from all the work at the hospital, but it's what I signed up for, so I'm good."

Despite my rattled nerves, we spend the rest of the ride chit-chatting before I drop him off at the gym.

As I walk into the hospital, I pray I don't see Levi before getting to the lab to grab some pregnancy test kits. I have to know and I have to know now.

After getting the test stick from the pharmacy, I drink all the water in my water bottle and head to the staff restroom. I make sure no one else is in any of the stalls before ripping open the test kit, my heart pounding away in my ears as I pee on it.

The five minutes I have to wait to know my fate is the longest five minutes I've ever waited in my life. I wasn't even this nervous when I was waiting to find out Mount Sinai's decision after I messed up Patrick Brenner's surgery.

When my timer goes off, I pick up the test stick.

Just look at it. You're either pregnant or you're not, no in-betweens.

I turn the test stick around and two bold pink lines stare back at me.

"Oh no no no," I say as a fresh wave of panic hits me.

I grab the second kit and force myself until some drops of pee come out. This time around, the five minutes go by really fast and when I look at the stick again, there are still two pink lines on it.

The first time around wasn't a fluke. I am pregnant. I am carrying Levi's baby.

Fuck my life! Only someone with my shitty luck would forget to take her pill on the same day she sleeps with a guy she really likes without protection.

What if Levi thinks I did this intentionally to trap him with a baby, or worse still what if he doesn't want this baby?

Being a failed neurosurgical resident and single mom at twenty-six wasn't part of my plan, but I should've known something like this would happen. My plans usually go to shit half the time.

As I exit the bathroom, I feel as numb as someone who's about to go under the knife and has been pumped full of anesthesia. That feeling quickly goes away when I see Levi walking toward me, a smile plastered across his face.

If only he knew I'm about to blow up his entire life, because not telling him isn't an option for me.

I feel like my insides have turned to jelly when we close in on each other.

"Just the person I wanted to see. This is Ken, from HR. I've been telling him about those ideas you've been talking about. Let's hear them."

I clear my throat. "Um, Dr. Greenwood, I'd like to speak to you in private if you don't mind."

I guess he can see the fear in my eyes because he quickly dismisses Ken from HR and asks me where I'd like to talk. We end up in his office and he sits beside me on the sofa.

"What's going on? You look like you've seen a ghost." I stay silent so he takes my hand and interlaces it in his. "Just tell me, that's the only way we'll get through it."

Keeping my eyes locked on him, I mutter the words "I...I...I'm pregnant."

His eyes widen in shock and he drops my hand. "How could this have happened? The first time we slept together, you told me you were on the pill, and the second time I used a condom just in case."

"I thought I was on the pill the first time, but I found out today that I had forgotten to take my pill that day."

"This is unbelievable, are you sure?"

I nod solemnly. "I'm three weeks and four days late and the two tests I did were both positive. Levi, I swear, you're the only man I've been with since I came back to Elvesridge. I can also assure you that I didn't want or plan for this to happen," I say, wiping away the tears flowing down my cheeks.

He sits beside me and takes my hands in his. "I believe you. It's okay. Everything is going to be okay."

"Really?"

"Yes. There are worse things that can happen than having a baby with the woman you love."

It's my eyes that are wide open in shock now. "You love me?"

He places my palm on his chest. "My heart may be racing this fast because you just told me I'm going to be a dad, but I couldn't be sure because this is how my heart races whenever you're around me. Seeing you instantly makes my day one thousand percent better no matter how awful it's been, and when I think of spending the rest of my life with you, this warmth takes over my entire body, rather than the freaked-out feeling the thought used to bring me in the past. I love you, Lilian Weatherby, I really do."

"Are you saying all this because I'm pregnant?"

"Well, it might have pushed me to say it sooner than I would have, but the truth is that if I'm being honest with myself, I've loved you since the day you called me a psycho."

A teary smile spreads over my face. "You don't know how long I've waited to hear you say you love me."

"Why?"

"Because I'm in love with you too."

Our lips meet and linger before he pulls me into a tight hug. I stay there, wishing that this moment would never end.

Chapter
Twenty-Two

♥

Levi

L ilian's head lying on my shoulder, knowing that our child is in her belly, and hearing her say she loves me—it feels like I'm in the middle of a dream, one that someone will come in any minute to wake me up from.

Unfortunately, I don't need anyone to wake me because I'm fully awake when I remember Aiden.

He is for sure going to kill me. Not only have I been sleeping with his sister, I lied to him about it and now she's pregnant with my child. I didn't just break our bro code, I ripped the book to shreds and set the pieces on fire.

Someone eventually does come to rouse us from our bliss—my assistant Sam informing me that we have tons of patients waiting to be seen.

Lilian and I brace ourselves for the crazy day ahead of us, and after we see our last patient for the day, I tell her that we need to talk.

"You don't look so good. Please don't tell me you've changed your mind about us."

"Never. I've been thinking about Aiden. He's my best friend and I've hated keeping us a secret from him all this time." I draw in a long breath and place my hand on her belly. "I think it's high time I came clean to him about us, all of us. In fact, I think it's time we tell your parents and everyone else about us too."

"Are you trying to give me a heart attack or something? Do you even know how uptight my parents are about such things? They got married as virgins and frown upon any form of sexual activity outside marriage. Don't you think they're going to flip the hell out when they find out their only daughter is pregnant?"

"You do know that your belly is going to grow rounder and rounder until you can't hide it anymore, right? Lily, I love you and I need Aiden and your parents to know this and to know that I intend to be there for you and our daughter or son every step of the way."

"You really mean that?"

"Every word. We'll deal with any blowback together okay? I'm certain it won't be that bad."

"Don't be too sure, you don't know my parents as well as I do."

"That's true, but I believe that no matter what, they love you and want what's best for you."

"Oh really? And you think you're what's best for me?"

I smile and kiss her. "I know I'm what's best for you."

"Fine, let's do this. I'll talk to them about inviting you to dinner this Friday and we'll see how things go from there."

I smile at her calmly. "That's great."

Despite my calm demeanor, in reality, I'm worried about Aiden and how he'll react to this news. But I know I have to man up and tell him myself. It may cost us our friendship but it's a risk I'm willing to take for the woman I love.

Oh wow, "the woman I love" has a nice ring to it. Anna called it, but I was too pigheaded to believe her.

I spend the next few days worried about what will happen when I meet Lily's parents. I'm worried about what they'll think of the age gap between us.

What if they feel I'm too old for her? I am, after all, ten years older than her.

Despite my worry, I'm excited to finally let them know how I feel about their daughter so we can stop sneaking around like high school lovers.

I'm so nervous that I need someone to talk to, so I call Anna.

"Hey bro, how are you?"

"I'm great. How are Shawn and my naughty niece and nephew?"

"We heard that," they both chorus.

"They can hear me?"

"Yeah. We're about to head to the store to pick up some ice cream because they did well in their midterms."

"Well done, kids."

"Thanks, Uncle Levi."

"So you aren't driving yet?"

"No, I was just about to pull out of the driveway."

"Can you step out of the car for a second?"

"Okay...I'll be right back, kids," Anna says, and I hear the door shut behind her. "I'm out of the car. Is this about Dad?"

"No, it's about me. I told Lilian I loved her yesterday."

"Lilian, your research partner and physician's assistant?"

"One and the same."

"And what was her response?"

"She told me she loves me too."

"Yes!" Anna shrieks. "I knew there was something special between you two. This is great news."

"That's not all...she's pregnant."

"What? Don't fuck with me right now."

"I'm not fucking with you. She's carrying my baby."

"And you're sure it's yours?"

"Yes. She told me it's mine and I trust her one-hundred-percent."

"So what you're saying is that soon you're going to be a father and I'll be an auntie?"

"That's how it works."

"This is huge. How are you feeling?"

"Honestly? I'm freaking out. It's not like we had the best example growing up."

"It doesn't matter. The way you are with kids, especially mine, is exceptional. You're going to be the best dad. I'm sure of it."

"Thank you. I just hope Aiden and her parents feel the same way."

"Aiden doesn't know yet?"

"No, and I'm worried he won't take it well."

"Look, bro, you love her and you want to be there for her and the baby. If they don't see how great that is, then that's on them. I'm so happy for you, Lev. You deserve this."

"Thanks, sis."

"I'm going to be the best auntie the world has ever seen. I'll for sure spoil that kid rotten. Can I tell Shawn and the kids?"

"Fine, tell them."

"They're going to be so excited. Bye."

"Bye."

When Lilian tells me on Friday that she's spoken to her parents and they have invited me for dinner that evening, my anxiety skyrockets a thousand percent.

She told them the dinner was to officially thank me for giving her a job at Greenwood Hospital, so they don't have a clue what we intend to do.

I must have changed my shirt a hundred times before settling for a gray shirt and navy blue pants. I have to remind myself that what I wear to the dinner won't in any way determine how Aiden and Lilian's parents react to our news.

On second thought, maybe I should wear black to hide the blood stains in case Aiden decides to kill me.

When I drive up to the Weatherby mansion, I find Lilian pacing the garden, a frightened look on her face.

I quickly exit the car and walk over to her, stopping her in her tracks with a hug.

"Hey, baby, you need to relax, okay?" I lower my voice. "This can't be good for the baby. Relax, just breathe."

She inhales deeply and expels the air through her mouth.

"I need you to know that no matter what happens in there, I love you and we're going to be okay."

She nods, her demeanor a lot calmer. "Okay."

I take her hand in mine and we walk into the house together, only letting go of each other's hand as we enter the dining area.

"Good evening, Ethan and Grace," I say, as Lilian's parents get up to greet me.

"Good evening, my good man. I'm sorry we didn't do this sooner," Ethan says, taking my hand in a firm handshake while I kiss Grace on the cheek.

"Hey man," Aiden greets me, signaling me to take the empty seat next to him.

Bad idea. I want to be as far away from Aiden *as possible when we break the news, not seated next to him.*

"Let's eat," Ethan announces, and the servers start us off with some salad and creamy tomato soup.

Everything looks so good and I'm sure it tastes as good as it looks. Too bad I can't enjoy the baked salmon and garlic mashed potatoes because my stomach has been in knots since I sat down.

The last thing I want to do is engage in any of the conversations flying around at the dinner table, but I don't want to make Lilian any more uncomfortable than she looks so I strike up conversations like it's my favorite thing to do.

After some time, the servers return with some slices of apple pie and when we're done with that, I figure I could use more liquid courage so I pour the rest of my Chardonnay down my throat.

I give Lilian, who's sitting across from me, a look that lets her know that I'm ready. She nods in agreement.

"Mom, Dad, Aiden. Levi and I have something important to tell you." Every eye in the room is on her as she continues. "I don't think there's a gentler way to say this so here goes—I'm pregnant and Levi is the father."

Aiden's fork clatters loudly onto his plate. "What the hell are you talking about?"

"Levi and I have been seeing each other since I came back into town. It wasn't planned, we unexpectedly fell for each other, one thing led to another and here we are."

Aiden turns his head to face me and the disbelief in his eyes is clear as day. "This is a sick joke, right? Tell me it's a joke and I'll believe you."

"I'm sorry, man, but it's the truth, Lilian and I are in love and she's carrying my baby."

He stares at me, fury and disappointment simmering in his eyes. Out of nowhere, he gets up and throws his plate of unfinished pie across the room, making everyone jump in fear.

"Jesus, Aiden, take it easy," I say, standing up to face him.

"How dare you tell me to take it easy? You were fooling around with my sister behind my back and blatantly lying to my face all along. We had a deal that we would never touch each other's sister, but I guess I'm the fool who took it seriously and I guess fifteen years of friendship means nothing to you."

"Come on, Aiden, you know that's not true."

"Let me tell you what's true. Our friendship is over and you're as good as dead to me. As for you, Lil, I can't even look at you right now," he says, shoving me to the side as he walks away from us.

"Aiden, please," Lilian calls out to him. When he doesn't come back, she faces her parents. "Mom? Dad? You've been awfully quiet, please say something."

"I can't believe you would do something like this. Getting pregnant from your brother's best friend is a new low, even for you," Grace says, shaking her head in disapproval.

"I'm sorry, but I'm with your mom on this one. I had hoped you'd try to get your life together and fix whatever you screwed up in New York, but I now see that I bet on the wrong horse. I wanted so much better for you, Lily, and this is going to break Gramps and Nana's hearts."

I look at Lilian and the look on her face is just gut-wrenching.

"Mr. and Mrs. Weatherby, I know you're angry, but I want to assure you that I love your daughter very deeply and I intend to be there for her and the baby."

"Since you love her so much, she can live with you, because we don't want whatever this is in our home," Grace says, getting up to leave.

"I'm sorry," Ethan mutters, following closely behind her.

I walk around the table and gather a now hysterically sobbing Lilian into my arms.

"Oh baby, I'm sorry. I'm so sorry."

Chapter
Twenty-Three

♥

Lilian

After my parents storm out, Levi holds me in his arms till I stop sobbing and regain my composure. Mom being disappointed in me is nothing new, even my birth feels like a disappointment to her at this point, but never in a million years did I think I'd see that same look mirrored on Dad's face.

"Are you sure you'll be okay spending the night here?" Levi asks as I walk him to his car almost fifteen minutes after dinner.

"It's going to be a long night for sure, but I'll manage. The last thing I want is everyone waking up tomorrow morning and I'm not home."

"I understand, and I believe that by morning, everyone will have cooled off and will be more open to talking with you. You guys will work this out."

"I hope so."

***

Unfortunately, Levi couldn't have been more wrong. At first, I thought Mom and Dad were just upset and would eventually come around, but days pass and they still aren't talking to me.

To make matters worse, when Gramps and Nana find out, they tell me in no uncertain terms how disappointed they are by what I've done. They believed they had set a good example and model for what a healthy long-term relationship could look like, instead of the excuse for pre-marital and unprotected sex it's become these days.

Like with Dad, Gramps and Nana have never been disappointed in me before. Aiden is often the one at the receiving end of their disapproving glares, and it feels like someone has taken a dagger to my heart.

The only person who could make this whole situation a little more bearable for me is Aiden, but he's angrier at me than everyone else is.

I've made several attempts to explain to him that Levi and I never meant to hurt or lie to him, but he has refused to talk to me, let alone listen to reason.

Having exhausted all my options, I resort to paying for a class at his gym because I know he won't want to leave mid-workout, which means he will have no choice but to talk to or at least listen to me.

"What are you doing here?" he asks when he sees me, not bothering to mask the annoyance in his voice.

I mount one of the bikes. "I decided to come here since you've refused to talk to me at home."

"Go home, Lilian. We don't have anything to talk about," he says, loading some weight onto his weight bars.

"Yes we do, I need to explain some things to you."

"Like what? How I helped you find a job in my best friend's hospital and the only way you saw fit to thank me was by sleeping with him and getting pregnant? Did I cover it or is there anything else you want to add?"

"Aiden, you know that's not who I am."

"Actually, the past few days have revealed that I don't know you. I guess New York changed you more than I cared to admit. Do you know what the most painful part of this whole thing is? You had multiple opportunities to tell me but you chose to lie straight to my face. I'm sure you and Levi had a good laugh about how gullible I was."

"On the contrary, Levi was very worried about how you'd react when you found out about us, we both were. And judging by the way you're acting right now, we were right to keep it from you."

"Oh, that's great. I feel so much better knowing you two were on the same page to make a fool out of me," he says, putting in his AirPods—a sign that we're done talking—and proceeding to lift his weights.

When I see that he's not interested in anything I have to say, I change into my work clothes and head for the hospital.

As soon as Levi lays his eyes on me, he pulls me into the conference room. "Did you get any sleep last night? You look exhausted."

"I don't think I've gotten any proper sleep in days. Everyone is just so upset with me, especially Aiden and my grandparents."

"Okay, that's it. You're coming to stay with me and you're not going back home until they have a change of heart."

I shake my head no. "That will make everything so much worse."

"I don't care. My priority right now is keeping you and our unborn child as happy and safe as I can, which means I can't allow you to remain in that house."

From the look on Levi's face, I can tell that he's really worried about me. "Alright. I'll go home and pick up some of my stuff after work."

"There's no need for that. Anna left some of her clothes behind when she moved to Chicago, and the two of you are the same size. If you need anything else, I'll get it for you."

"And your dad? Are you sure he's okay with me coming to stay at your place?"

"It's my house, he doesn't have a choice."

When we get to the house later that evening, Levi introduces me to his staff and they welcome me wholeheartedly. As we go in, I see Dr. William on the couch leisurely scrolling through television channels.

"Good evening, Dr. William, how do you do?"

"I'm doing well," he says, flashing me a welcoming smile.

I look over at Levi and he's as surprised as I am at his father's reaction to my presence.

"I want to apologize for my behavior when I came to visit the hospital."

"There's no need for that, Dr. William. All is forgiven."

"I'm glad to hear that, and please call me William."

"Did you use some sort of voodoo or juju I don't know about on your dad?" I ask Levi as we go up the stairs.

"I told him how important you are to me and I guess he listened."

We get into the room and seeing his bed takes me back to the last time we were here. I look over at him—given how flushed his cheeks are, I'm sure he's remembering the same thing I am.

After I settle in, he gives me Anna's already dry-cleaned clothes and they fit perfectly. He also hands me a bag of personal effects he sent one of the housekeepers to get for me.

The next morning when I wake up, I don't see Levi on the bed or anywhere in the room. Checking my phone, I see that there are no missed calls from Aiden or my parents. Either they don't know that I didn't come home last night, or they do and don't care.

Despite being sad about that, I know that Levi was right about bringing me here. I had a great night's sleep for the first time in days and I'm ready and energized for the day.

"What do you think you're doing?" Levi asks as he walks into the room with a tray of assorted fruits which he drops on the bed.

"Getting ready to go to work."

"Oh no you're not," he says, gently nudging me onto the bed and turning on the television. "You're going to stay in bed, eat these fruits, and watch some movies until I get back later this evening. Doctor's orders."

"But what about the hospital and our patients?" I protest.

"They'll be there when you get back."

"And who will assist you with them?"

"I've already spoken to Dr. Thorne and she loaned me Laura for the day."

"You know she has a massive crush on you, right? And you look exceptionally hot today."

"Doesn't matter if she's in love with me, I only have eyes for you," he says, capturing my lips with his soft ones. "The chef is making you some breakfast and I've told the housekeepers to ensure you have everything you need. I'll see you this evening," he says, leaving before I can get a word in.

I can't remember the last time I spent an entire day in bed being catered to hand and foot, but it's really relaxing. The only thing bothering me is the fact that no one from my family has called. I mean, they must have noticed that I'm still not home from work.

My phone rings and I grab it faster than the flash, hoping it's Aiden or my dad, but it's Anna calling me via video call which I feel is weird. I answer anyway.

"Hi, Anna."

"Lilian, hey. How are you feeling? I heard my brother placed you on a mandatory bed rest. Yes, I know you and Levi are together and that you're pregnant," she explains when she sees my surprised expression.

"I'm glad Levi told you."

"Yeah, me too. I'm excited about it and I'm sorry your family doesn't feel the same way."

I sigh deeply. "I just don't get why they're so upset."

"I kinda get it. No matter your age, you're still their little girl and they want the best for you. You'll understand when you become a parent."

I instinctively rub my belly. "I guess I will."

"It doesn't matter, because I'm excited enough for all of them and I'm glad I'm getting an amazing sister-in-law."

"What do you mean sister-in-law? Levi and I aren't getting married anytime soon, we're taking things slow."

"Oh really? You might want to look at your door."

"What are you talking about?" I ask, looking toward the door.

Just then, the door opens and Levi walks straight toward me on the bed.

"Hey baby, what are you doing back so soon? Did you forget something?"

My hands fly to my mouth when he pulls out a tiny box containing a huge diamond ring and goes down on one knee beside the bed.

"I know it may seem a bit sudden, and this is probably not the proposal you dreamed of, but I'm sure—no, I'm certain that I want to spend the rest of my life with you. That's if you'll have me. Lilian Rose Weatherby, will you marry me?"

"I can't believe this is happening," I say, my whole body shaking as I slowly get up from the bed.

"Will you marry me?" he asks again, and I quickly collect my thoughts.

"Yes, baby, of course I'll marry you," I say, and he gets up and slides the ring on my finger. "It's perfect." I wipe at the tears flowing down my face as I look at the ring on my finger in disbelief.

"And that's not all. I have a surprise for you."

"Baby, I don't think I can handle another surprise."

He picks up the TV remote and switches it to music mode, then presses play.

"Wait a minute! Oh my God! Is this from Flaming Lips yet to be released album 'Rock my Soul'?" He affirms my question with a nod. "Shut the front door. How did you get it?"

He closes the space between us and pulls my body to his, interlocking our fingers on one hand and placing the other around my waist. "I called in a favor."

"How did I get so lucky?" I ask as we sway to the music filtering through the speakers.

"Luck didn't stand a chance when I met you."

"Gosh, you always know the right thing to say," I moan, my lips crashing into his in desperate hunger.

Anna clears her throat as a reminder she's still here. "My work here is done, so I'm gonna leave you two lovebirds alone now."

"Thanks, Anna," we both sing.

As soon as she ends the call, we rip each other's clothes off and make love passionately with Flaming Lips playing in the background.

The perfect finish to a perfect moment.

Chapter
Twenty-Four

♥

Levi

It's been a week since Lilian and I got engaged and I've been telling anyone who cared to listen.

Shockingly when I tell my dad, he seems happy that I've finally gotten someone to put up with my arrogant ass. His words, not mine. Which is ironic since he's more of an ass than I am.

When we announce our engagement in the hospital, everyone is happy, except maybe for Laura. She keeps a long face and snaps at everyone all day but soon she gets over it and wishes us all the best.

Despite putting on a brave face, I can tell that Lilian is not completely happy. And I don't need a soothsayer to tell me why she's unhappy.

I've tried reaching out to Aiden multiple times so we can talk and sort things out, but he's been adamantly against hearing anything I have to say. Things have been awkward between us at the gym, but ours is the only well-equipped gym in town so neither of us can quit.

If it were up to me, I'd let Aiden take his time and forgive me whenever he's ready, but I'm sick of seeing Lilian so upset about her family's rejection and I need to do something about it before the wedding.

The wedding plans have been in full swing because Lily wants to get married before her baby bump becomes visible. So I have to get Aiden to hear me out sooner rather than later.

All I need is a plan to make sure he has no choice but to hear me out. I convince Maureen to help me set up a meeting with Aiden, and she's all too eager to help.

When Aiden shows up at the Moonlite Diner and sees me instead of Maureen who he thinks he's meeting for a surprise dinner date, he's furious. He immediately turns around to leave but I grab his hand and stop him.

"Look, man, I know you're angry with me, but if you still care about your sister one bit, you'll sit and hear me out."

I know how hard it is for him, but eventually Aiden pulls out his chair and sits down. "What about my sister? How has she been?"

"She's good. We got engaged."

His head jerks up from the menu in his hand. "You did? When?"

"A week today."

"Wow, this thing between you two is really serious isn't it?"

I look him square in the eyes. "I promise you that I'm crazy about her. After Stella, I never thought I would like, let alone love anyone again, but Lily came along and proved me wrong. I know my love for her made you feel like I betrayed our pact to not date each other's sister and I'm sorry, but I never meant for it to happen. It just did."

He lets out a sigh. "I guess I overreacted. You've been my friend for almost fifteen years now and I should've known you wouldn't do anything to hurt Lily. Besides, we made the *siblings out-of-bounds* pact in high school. It's irrational for me to keep holding on to it this strongly."

"I'm really glad you feel this way, man. Our wedding is coming up in two weeks and I'd love for you and your folks to be there."

"Isn't two weeks too soon?"

"That's the way Lilian wants it. And it's going to be a very small ceremony. Just family and a few friends, so why waste time?"

"I'll try and talk to my family, convince them to come to the wedding."

"I know that would make Lilian very happy."

"So, where's my little sister? I would love to congratulate her in person."

"She's at my place right now and I know she would love that."

When we get home, I find Lilian in the kitchen getting some frozen fruit popsicles which is the only thing she's been able to keep down since her morning sickness started.

"Hey, baby. There's someone here to see you."

"What? You should have told me you were bringing someone home with you. I look a mess."

"Trust me, it won't matter."

"Hey, Lily."

She stops in her tracks when she sees him.

"Aiden!" She drops the popsicle and runs into his arms. They hug and hold each other for a few minutes. "It's so good to see you. I missed you so much, T."

"I missed you too, Lil. The house hasn't quite been the same without you. I'm sorry for being such a tool."

"I get it, you were just trying to look out for me."

"So I hear you're getting hitched?"

She nods enthusiastically and I can see how happy she is that Aiden is here.

"I'm happy for you, sis."

"Thanks, bro."

I pour a glass of wine and some sparkling apple juice which I hand to Aiden and Lilian.

"So since your parents have refused to speak to us, I'd like to officially ask for your permission to marry your sister."

"Dude, she said yes. That's all the permission you need," Aiden says, and we all laugh.

"It's great you two are friends again."

I agree with a nod. "Yeah, it was weird not talking to you at the gym."

"Bro, I had to work out with creepy Larry."

"Oh no."

Aiden pulls his face into a grimace. "Oh yes, more than once."

***

After two weeks of intense planning and execution, our wedding day is finally here. As I look into my home garden which has been transformed into a gorgeous intimate wedding space, I see my niece and nephew—who will be flower girl and ring bearer—running around the garden.

The arch under which Lilian and I will say our vows is decorated with lilies and lilac flowers and surrounded by other floral arrangements. Many guests are already seated and I notice there are way more people than we had wanted.

Just then Aiden walks in and pats me on the shoulder. "How are you feeling, my man?"

"Nervous...but excited."

"That's good."

"Why are there so many people, man? We said only family and friends."

"You're marrying a Weatherby, these are family and friends."

"I see your parents couldn't make it though?"

"Nah, I know my dad wanted to come, but my mom knows how to hold a grudge and sadly she calls the shots."

"I better go check in on Lilian and see how she's doing."

"Don't worry, I've got it. You just worry about saying the correct name up there."

"Haha. Very funny."

In about forty-five minutes, everything is set and I'm standing beside the minister under the arch, waiting for my bride-to-be.

Anna and Laura, the only bridesmaids, walk up and join me in front and then Lilian appears on the walkway, her hand draped over Aiden's as he walks her down the aisle. She looks pristine in her crystal white wedding dress, her face slightly hidden underneath her veil.

As she gets to me, I uncover her face and a "wow" escapes my lips. "You've never looked more beautiful than you do right now."

She flashes me the most beautiful smile. "And you've never had more hair gel than you do right now."

My mouth widens in mock shock. "Oh, wow. You're so mean."

"Ready whenever you are," the reverend says, a little amused by our banter.

"We're ready," we both say, our eyes fixated on each other.

"Dearly beloved, we are gathered here today in the presence of family and friends to join Lilian Weatherby and Levi Greenwood together in holy matrimony…"

***

Sitting on this side of the fence feels weird to me. I look around and there are a few other people huddled together in solidarity, waiting for someone—which is usually me—to come through one of the OR's swinging doors and tell them if their loved one made it out of surgery or not.

But today, it's my turn to wait and I fucking hate it.

Lilian went into labor last night and everything was going smoothly till the early hours of this morning when she experienced sudden severe abdominal pain followed by heavy vaginal bleeding.

Dr. Barner, Greenwood Hospital's resident obstetrician, immediately flagged it as a uterine rupture and suggested that an emergency cesarean section be done to get the baby out to prevent oxygen deprivation leading to birth asphyxia, and also to repair the uterus.

I was asked to stay back as they wheeled her off for surgery and the wait has been the longest of my life. I need to remind myself to be gentler with families of patients next time because not knowing what's going on with your loved one is hellish.

I waited for almost thirty minutes before it dawned on me to call Aiden and inform him about Lilian's situation. He assured me he was coming to the hospital right away but he's not yet here and I'm getting restless.

Whenever the swinging door opens, everyone's eyes go to the door in anticipation, watching to see if the doctor will walk toward them.

The hospital doors swing open and I look up to see Aiden walk in. He starts toward me and to my great surprise, his mom, dad, and my dad are with him.

"Hi Ethan, Grace...hey Dad."

"Levi," Grace responds, taking my hand. "How's Lilian? Have you gotten any updates from the doctors?"

"Not yet, but I'm sure that any moment now, he'll come out and tell us how she is. She'll be quite overjoyed to see you guys, that I know for sure."

"It's okay, son. She'll be alright. You'll see," Dad says, patting me firmly on the back.

"Thanks, Dad."

We don't have to wait too long before the doors open and Dr. Barner approaches us.

I get up when I see him coming. "How are my wife and son doing?"

"It was tough, but we managed to resuscitate the baby after delivery and repair the uterine rupture. Mother and son are doing great. Congratulations, Dr. Greenwood."

"Thank you very much, Dr. Barner. Thanks for keeping my family safe. Can we see her now?"

"She's still unconscious, but you can go in alone and only for a few minutes. We need to give her some time to rest, she has been through a lot. You can see your baby though, he's in the hospital's nursery."

After he leaves, we all rush over to the nursery and my beautiful baby boy is lying in one of the cribs. I approach his bed and pick him up for the first time since he was born and a sudden wave of emotions hits me.

Aiden, Ethan, and Grace surround me, all fawning over the baby.

"Can I hold him?" Grace asks, and I gently hand him over to her.

"So, what's my grandson's name? Did you guys decide yet?"

"Not yet. I need to go see Lilian now," I say, leaving them in the nursery.

When I walk into Lilian's room, she's lying on the bed looking angelic in her hospital gown. I take the seat beside her bed and hold her hands in mine.

"Hey, baby. How are you holding up? I thought you'd like to know that our son is here and he is so beautiful. I still can't believe we created something so beautiful and I know you can't wait to see and hold him, so wake up soon okay?"

I bend my head to kiss her hand and it's barely a whisper but I hear it very clearly. "Levi..."

"Oh my God, baby, you're awake," I say, giving her a soft kiss.

"How's our son doing?"

"He's doing great, he's so beautiful."

"I heard," she says weakly. "Can I see him?"

"Certainly. I'll go get him along with some other people who want to see you."

I leave the room, returning shortly with the baby and handing him over to Lilian who bursts into tears.

"You were right, he's so beautiful."

"That he is. So, have we decided on a name yet?"

She nods. "Gabriel Lumière Greenwood."

"That's perfect," I say, kissing her again. I signal to her family to come in. "Look who's here to see you."

"Mom! Dad! You came?" Lilian asks, fresh tears welling up in her eyes.

"Of course we did, baby girl, and we are eight months too late. Do you think you can ever forgive us?" Grace asks, holding Ethan's hand.

"I forgive you, Mom. You too, Dad. I love you both so much."

"We love you too, honey," Ethan says, placing a kiss on her forehead.

My phone rings almost immediately and it's an unknown number so I pick up. "Hello?"

"Is this Dr. Levi Greenwood?"

"This is he."

"We're calling you from NIH. We've finally decided on your research. We've approved it and allocated fifty thousand dollars to it for starters."

"What? No way! Today couldn't possibly get any better."

I turn to face the room. "Hey baby, that was the NIH. Our research funding has been approved."

"Oh my God, Levi, that's amazing."

"But not as amazing as everyone being here. Anna's flying in tomorrow with her family too. I love you guys so much."

"I'm so proud of you, son, and I know your mom would've been prouder," Dad says, pulling me into an embrace.

"Love you, Dad."

"Love you too, son."

Chapter
Twenty-Five

Lilian

"Hey baby," I say, lying in bed next to Levi.

"Hey," he replies, pulling me close to him till I'm cradled in his arms. "Thank God he's finally asleep."

"Yeah, that was rough. Can you believe it's been six months already?"

"No, it feels just like yesterday. They grow up so fast don't they?"

"They really do. How's the research going?" I ask, looking at the pile of files on our nightstand.

"It's going great. I had a significant breakthrough yesterday."

"That's great to hear, you've been working so hard on this."

"What's going on? You sound like something's bothering you."

"How do you always know that?"

"Cause I know you. So what's up?" he asks, closing the laptop in front of him.

"I've been doing some thinking, and I believe I'm ready to continue my neurosurgery residency."

He slightly adjusts himself to look me square in the face. "Are you serious?"

"I am."

"That's amazing. What made you change your mind? The last we spoke of it, you weren't sure."

"Amelia. Her case touched me in a way I never imagined. It helped me reaffirm that helping people through difficult health situations is my path in life. I've given this a lot of thought and I know that now may not be the perfect time with Gabriel being six months old, and you busy with your—-"

He cuts me off with a kiss. "Now is the perfect time. I can double up my efforts with helping with the baby. Your parents and cousins can also help with Gabriel, they've been offering to babysit him since he was born. Babe, I'm so happy you decided to do this. You were born to be a neurosurgeon."

"Thanks, babe. For being an amazing husband and father, for everything."

"You make it very easy. Oh, lest I forget, I have a surprise for you."

"Surprise?"

I watch as he sifts through the files on the nightstand, pulls out a piece of paper, and hands it to me. I have a confused look on my face as I read through the paper in my hand.

"This is a lease agreement for a property?"

"Yes. It's for our new music studio."

I sit up on the bed. "What? Oh no you didn't!"

"I did. You've been wishing that Elvesridge had a music studio where the talent of some of the singers who auditioned for the singing competition could be honed. And so I thought who better to open a studio and hone these young talents if not us? That's if you're interested."

"Are you kidding? Of course I'm interested. I've wanted this since I was a teenager belting out songs while having a bath. Thank you so much, babe."

"Oh no no," Levi says, planting a kiss on my neck. "I just spent a lot of money on this studio and I'm going to need a bit more than *thank you*."

I smile. "Oh really? What do you want exactly?"

He lifts my top and kisses me across my CS scar.

"I hate when you do that."

He raises his head to look at me. "Why?"

"Because it's ugly."

He pulls back and looks straight at me. "Baby, you got it from bringing a whole human life into our world. It's many things, but ugly isn't and will never be one of them."

"Okay, that's it. Come do whatever you want to me."

He lowers his head to my lips and as his lips touch mine, tingling sensations flood my entire body. I know without a doubt that this is where I belong. I am home.

***

A month later, with help from friends and family members, especially Aiden who helped put up all the necessary equipment, Lumière Studios is fully operational and we're ready to open our doors to the town.

"Hey babe," Levi says when he walks out of the back room.

"Hey."

"Everything looks so good."

"Yeah, right? Aiden truly has the magic touch."

"Are we good to go?"

"All good. Just waiting for our first student to walk through the door."

I barely finish my statement when the door opens and our first student walks in carrying her guitar and writing pad.

"Our very first student," I whisper to Levi. "So exciting."

Levi waves at her. "Hi, welcome to Lumière Studios. You can come in and close the door."

"I just wanted to be sure I had the right place." She peeks her head out of the door. "Hurry up guys, it's open."

Levi and I look at each other in amazement as a lot of people start coming into the studio. They keep walking in till there's no space left and we have to ask some people to go home and return tomorrow.

"We'll have to come up with a better system to make sure no one misses out," I say to Levi after he shows our last intake of the day to his seat.

"As soon as possible, and we'll need to hire someone to help out because this is crazy."

"I don't even recognize some of the faces in here. Do you?"

Levi shakes his head no. "I think they may be from neighboring towns."

"That's awesome. This is a dream come true, and I'm glad I get to experience it with you."

"Me too, babe."

Epilogue — Six Months Later

♥

Lilian

"Hey kids, slow down. You don't want to fall and hurt yourselves," I yell out to Sam and Emilia as I set Gabriel's birthday cake on the center table.

"The cake looks so good," Anna says, putting some drinks around it.

"Thanks, Anna. Do you know where Gabriel is?"

"Last I saw him, he was with Dad."

"He's especially fond of him isn't he?"

Anna smiles. "Yes. I've never seen Dad quite so taken with anyone. Not even Emilia or Sam. I'm happy Gabriel is bringing him so much joy in this delicate phase of his life."

"Me too."

"How's the residency going?"

"It's been tough, especially doing it while caring for Gabriel, but your brother has been an angel through it all. I'm really lucky to have him."

"Oh please. He's the lucky one and he knows it."

"Could you help me grab the candles? They're on the kitchen counter."

"You got it."

As I look around, I notice that everyone is here for Gabriel's first birthday—even Joyce, my cousin, is here with her cute cat.

Seeing everyone talking and sharing laughs makes me so happy. All I ever wished for was for my kids to grow up feeling the love of family, which is what Gabriel now has.

"Alright, everyone, gather around. It's time to cut the cake and open presents."

Everyone gathers around and Gabriel grabs onto my leg with his tiny hands so I pick him up. We all sing the Happy Birthday song to him and with my help, he cuts his cake.

"Alright. Which present shall we open first? I think we should start with mine. Daddy, would you mind helping Gabriel open his first present?"

"Not at all," Levi says, picking up the wrapped box with "From Mom" boldly written on it. He carefully unwraps it and opens the box inside. Lying there is a pregnancy test stick with two red lines.

He looks up at me. "Is this what I think it is?"

I give him a confirmatory nod.

"You're pregnant?" he asks, drawing everyone's attention toward me.

"Yes, I just found out last week."

"Oh my God!" he says, pulling Gabriel and me into a hug. "I'm going to be a father again?"

"Yes, you are."

"This is the best news ever."

Everyone gathers around us offering their congratulatory hugs and handshakes. As Anna helps our son unwrap the rest of his presents, Levi takes my hand in his.

"I didn't think I could be any happier than I was this morning, but you just proved me wrong. I love you so much and I hope you never doubt it."

"I love you too, baby."

THE END

Did "*Off-Limits Grumpy Doctor*" captivate you? Get ready for the journey of this ex-hockey star turned musician heartthrob, Holt Walter, who finds a second chance at love with his personal assistant. Hold on for an intense emotional escapade in this billionaire boss enemies-to-lovers tale, coming soon in my next release.

Meanwhile, meet our cabin crew Evelyn and our billionaire boss Alexander on this enemies to lovers, fake marriage and surprise pregnancy romance. So buckle your seatbelts and prepare for a heartwarming and turbulence-filled flight in *"Faking It With My Ex's Brother"*. Turn to the very next page to read Chapter One.

Sneak Peek

♥

Faking It With My Ex's Brother

I never pictured ending my wedding day heartbroken, certainly not in my ex-fiancé's brother's bed.

This jerk cheated on me with my best friend—a bride's worst nightmare.

Alone in my white dress, I drown myself at the bar next to a stranger in a gray suit.

But Alexander Grant isn't any ordinary stranger, he's my ex's brother.

Sharing my revenge scheme with him isn't on the agenda.

He offered his help, and our wild night made me forget the betrayal.

After that night, my world takes a surprising turn.

Alexander is now my new boss and working together isn't easy.

Yet he proposes a fake marriage to secure his inheritance.

And I get an irresistible pay in return.

But our pretense complicates *everything*.

Despite our constant bickering, genuine emotions simmer, and undeniable chemistry grows.

Faking it with my ex's brother is tough…especially now that I love him and—I'm pregnant.

Scan QR Code to start reading "Faking It With My Ex's Brother"!

Chapter One

Evelyn

I'd pictured my wedding day many times over the years, but my dreams had never ended with me at a bar, alone, desperate, and heart-broken—and most certainly not with me in bed with my fiancé's elder brother.

As Steph had put the finishing touches on my makeup earlier that day, my bridesmaids and maid of honor, Kim, were gushing over me like I was a princess about to say "I do" to her prince.

I'd picked up my phone to take a picture and a text from Daniel popped up on my screen:

I need you one last time, come to my room.

I smiled, desire coursing through me as I opened the text to send a reply, but my smile vanished instantly as my eye caught another text which read: *"I think Evelyn knows something, let's be more careful."*

Intrigued, I scrolled down and saw more raunchy texts I didn't remember sending to Daniel. I turned the phone around to see it was Kim's, temporarily knocking the breath out of my lungs. We had the same phone and phone case, but hers had her initials on it.

From the look on her face, it was clear she knew what I had found.

"Lyn, I can explain..." she started, but I didn't stick around to hear whatever inconsequential excuse she was about to feed me.

Throwing her phone across the room, I gathered my Oscar de la Renta custom gown—which had cost me an arm and a leg—and fled the room.

A voice that sounded like Kim's kept calling out for me to stop.

But I didn't stop.

I couldn't.

Grabbing my keys and jumping into my car, I drove away leaving a cloud of dust behind. I was desperate to get as far away from their betrayal as possible.

As I drove around Miami with no particular destination in mind, I cursed the day I'd met Daniel. It had been my third flight as a flight attendant, and he had been sitting in first class. Love at first sight was something I'd believed only happened in fairy tales, but that was the only way to describe our connection from the moment we locked eyes.

Despite being a firm believer in someday finding the perfect man, falling madly in love, and living happily ever after, I had constantly been unlucky with love. From my first crush, Billy, who had only asked me out because of a bet with his friends that he couldn't date the nerdiest girl in school—to my college boyfriend, Paul, who I had discovered was dating me and three other girls at the same time while I'd gullibly assumed we were exclusive.

The fact that I'd believed my luck had changed and I had found my happily ever after with Daniel only made the reality that I was driving around looking for a bar to drown my sorrows on our wedding day even more gut-wrenching. The only thing that could ease the pain I was feeling was alcohol. Thankfully, Miami was littered with bars so finding one wasn't difficult.

Upon entering the bar, I found something else that was certain to make me feel better—right in front of me, wrapped up in an expensive gray suit. He was sitting on a barstool and our eyes met. It was Alexander Grant, Daniel's older brother.

Doesn't he live in London? How is he in Miami? He didn't come back for our wedding, Daniel didn't invite him.

Sleeping with him would certainly give Daniel a taste of his own medicine. It was an unexpected gift, and gifts shouldn't be questioned.

I walked to the bar and stood beside him. His face mirrored the look of concern on everyone else's face at seeing a bride, still in her wedding dress, in a bar.

"I just found out that my fiancé has been hooking up with my best friend and I'm looking to even the score," I blurted out, shocked at my bluntness.

He glanced at me. "I can certainly help with that."

I could tell he didn't recognize me, which wasn't surprising since he had practically alienated his whole family after he left for London.

"I'm Alexander. You?" he asked, confirming my theory that he had no clue who I was. "I should at least know the name of the woman I'm about to help get back at her fiancé."

"Evelyn," I replied tautly, making it clear that I was unwilling to divulge any more information about myself.

Pouring the remaining scotch in his glass down my throat gave me a little more courage. "Let's go before I change my mind."

"I'm lodged in a hotel just around the corner," he said, leading the way out of the bar.

As we walked to the hotel, I put one foot gingerly in front of the other, my heart pounding away in my chest. Was I really going to sleep with my ex-fiancé's brother?

Yes, Daniel had hurt me. He was the reason for the throbbing pain I currently felt in my chest, yet I had never been one to have random sexual encounters.

Despite the carefree "it's just sex" approach everyone seemed to have these days, sex was something I still considered sacred, only to be enjoyed in committed relationships. Kim often called me a prude and it was a badge I wore proudly.

I was so lost in thought that I didn't realize we had entered the hotel lobby. It was only when we stepped into the elevator that I became aware of my surroundings.

"Congratulations," a lady riding with us in the elevator threw at me, and I nodded politely.

From the way her face was lit up with a smile, I could tell she was like me—a sucker for love. She must have thought we'd just tied the knot. I was still in my wedding gown after all, and with Alexander's well-tailored, formfitting suit it wasn't too far-fetched to assume he was the groom.

"After you," Alexander said as the elevator came to a stop and he ushered me into a lushly decorated room with a double bed.

Without wasting one second as the door shut behind us, he drew me close to his chest, which felt hard as a rock, his aftershave serenading my nostrils as he took my mouth in his. It was as though he could hear me second-guessing my decision to go through with my bold request at the bar, and he didn't want to give me a chance to back out.

He was gentle at first, teasing me, trying to get me to open up, but then he became more greedy, more demanding—like he was my master and my lips were his prisoners.

Scanning his face as he momentarily broke our kiss, I noted that he bore no resemblance to Daniel, which was a relief. I was already feeling guilty enough as it was and I didn't need any other reminder that he wasn't a random stranger.

As he sucked on my neck with his soft lips, every thought of Daniel and his betrayal fled my mind. I gave in to the moment, to the sweet sensation of Alexander's lips and tongue on my neck and the familiar sensation it was rousing between my thighs.

He was no novice at this; for a moment I wondered how many women he'd seduced just as he was seducing me, only hoping that at least none of them had been a runaway bride like me.

He came back to my lips and this time I returned his kiss, surrendering myself completely to the pleasure waves flooding through my whole body. I moved closer to him, desperate to close any inch of space between us. As I tugged away at my gown's corset, he put his hands over mine and shook his head, stopping me from making any further move to untie the dress.

His eyes, clear and blue, didn't leave mine as he raised my gown and pulled down the thong I had carefully selected for what I'd thought was going to be my first night as a married woman. Taking my lips hostage again, he took me right then and there, against the pale yellow wall of the hotel room.

"Bed...now," I managed to mutter in between moans. Not that I wasn't enjoying being pinned to the wall like prey under its predator, but I was concerned that he would tire out soon enough. I wasn't plus-sized but I wasn't a size zero either.

He gripped my waist firmly with my legs still wrapped around him and made his way across the room like a gazelle, swift and steady as he moved us to the bed. Not waiting as much as a second to catch his breath, his lips were back on mine, his tongue darting into every corner of my mouth.

It had been a while since I'd been kissed that long and hard. Daniel had never been a fan of kissing, he viewed it more as something to get out of the way before the main event.

I lay beneath Alexander, moaning carelessly as he drove me crazy, igniting fires in parts of my body I'd never known fires could be ignited in. It didn't take long before my body gave in, shaking as intense waves of pleasure washed over me.

As if my body had signaled him, he let out a groan as he climaxed before momentarily collapsing on top of me, his breath raspy against my ears.

As soon as he rolled off me, regret washed over me, instantly taking the place of the sensational tingling I'd been feeling just moments before. I quickly pulled down my wedding dress, eager to cover my naked body.

What am I hiding? Wasn't he buried deep inside me seconds ago? Besides, covering up won't change or erase what happened between us.

After I'd covered up, I lay there still as a statue, hoping Alexander wasn't a pillow-talk-after-sex kind of guy. I couldn't bring myself to look over to his side till a light snore escaped his lips.

I turned and saw that he was fast asleep. He had a peaceful look on his face, nothing like the man who had just been hungrily devouring my body.

This was the perfect opportunity for me to slip out, not wanting any part of the morning after or an awkward conversation. I tiptoed across the room, careful not to make a sound as I picked my thong up off the floor and slipped it on. I tried to open the door quiet as a cat, but an unmistakably deep voice stopped me in my tracks.

"Leaving without saying goodbye? I like your style."

As I turned around, I could see the remnants of a smile vanishing from his face. In a split second, I saw Daniel—they had the same smile. Those guilt pangs came again, gnawing hard at my insides. I reminded myself that I had nothing to feel guilty about, but it didn't help much.

"Hope the score has been evened?"

"What?" I asked, staring at him blankly.

"With your fiancé, hope you got him back for cheating on you?"

I wanted to speak, but the lump in my throat wouldn't let me, so I gave him a nod and practically ran out of there.

Scan QR Code to download "Faking It With My Ex's Brother"

Author's Book Corner

♥

T hank you for continuously supporting my writing endeavors. If you enjoyed this journey, I'd love to stay connected. Follow me on my Amazon Author Page for the latest releases, exclusive content, and more surprises!

Scan the QR code below to join me on Amazon:

But that's not all! For sneak peeks, exclusive giveaways, and a front-row seat to all things, subscribe to Brandy Piker's Newsletter.

Scan the QR code below to subscribe:

Thank you for being part of this adventure. Can't wait to share more stories with you!

Printed in Great Britain
by Amazon